Big Ideas for Northwest
Small Gardens

Marty Wingate

Big Ideas for Northwest
Small Gardens

Marty Wingate

Photographs by **Jacqueline Koch**

SASQUATCH BOOKS
SEATTLE

Printed in Singapore by Star Standard Industries Pte Ltd.

Published by Sasquatch Books

Distributed by Publishers Group West

07 06 05 04   6 5 4 3 2

Cover and interior design: Karen Schober

Cover and interior photographs: Jacqueline Koch

Copy editor: Alice Copp Smith

Library of Congress Cataloging in Publication Data

Wingate, Marty.

    Big ideas for northwest small gardens / Marty Wingate ; photographs by Jacqueline
Koch.

      p. cm.

      ISBN 1-57061-275-7

      1. Gardening—Northwest, Pacific. 2. Landscape gardening—Northwest, Pacific. I. Title.

      SB453.2.N83 W56 2003

      635.9'09795—dc21   2002030203

Sasquatch Books

119 South Main Street

Suite 400

Seattle, Washington 98104

(206) 467-4300

www.SasquatchBooks.com

books@SasquatchBooks.com

Contents

For Leighton—best
editor
husband
friend.

—M. W.

To my mother, who got me into the garden in the first place.

—J. K.

Thanks to the many gardeners and friends who have helped us along the way and patiently waited for the results. We are particularly grateful to Lynn Lustberg, editor of Garden Showcase *magazine, and* Vancouver, B.C., garden designers Debra Warmerdam (who took an entire day to drive us around town) and Laura-Jean Kelly. Thanks also to the gardeners who willingly let us poke around in their gardens, photographing or merely absorbing the lovely atmosphere. Gardeners are always good for a chat.

Marty would particularly like to acknowledge the support of her family. They always knew I would do this someday—my mom, Laverne Polk, and my sister, Carolyn Lockhart, and brother, Ed Polk, and their families. Thanks to the great garden club ladies who provide endless inspiration—Jane Tobin, Jutta Rhinehart, and Dorothy Stapp. I am grateful to Mary Kate Parker and Mary Helbach for offering encouragement over countless cups of tea. And thanks to Ellen Morrison for her gentle suggestions that always made sense. Finally, a triple-shot mocha with extra whip goes to a fine photographer, Jacqueline.

Jacqueline would like to say many thanks to those who put me up, or rather put up with me, for many nights on their couches, futons, or guest beds: Timothy and Soraya, Miracle and Andrew, Bob and Wendy, Donna, and Elizabeth in Vancouver. And thanks to Chris for having food and a hot tub waiting for me when I got home.

Finally, thanks to the editors and designers at Sasquatch who took our words and photos and brought them to life on these pages.

—Marty Wingate and Jacqueline Koch

Left: **Small gardens are multipurpose. Here, the plantings around a low picket fence include flowers for cutting, such as roses and peonies, in addition to fillers, such as hardy geraniums, which bloom throughout the summer.**

Right: **The outside world often intrudes on small gardens, but here the climbing rose 'Commitment' holds its own with municipal signage.**

Introduction

Small gardens inspire adjectives such as "charming," "sweet," and "diminutive." Large gardens get described as "expansive," "bold," or "dynamic." It's no wonder that we gardeners with small spaces sometimes feel as if we're being patted on the head and told, "Aren't you just the cutest thing?"

We don't help ourselves when we try to reproduce a large garden in a small space, so we must adapt what we want to what we have. We may not have room to hide an entire cutting garden out of view, so we must tuck our cutting flowers into the whole scheme of the garden (and also be inventive about what goes into a vase of "flowers"). The 10-foot-deep-by-100-foot-long border can handle fifty different kinds of plants with room for repetition and a flow of color. The small garden with fifty different kinds of plants in its 6-by-10 "border" looks like a cake with multicolored candy sprinkles on it. And those of you who don't think that fifty plants can fit into 60 square feet have already given yourselves away—you don't have a small garden.

In the maritime Northwest, as in other parts of the country, the garden usually divides into smaller areas, especially when the house sits smack in the middle of the property. If the house sits back or forward on the property, then the front garden probably has more room than the back or vice versa. There may be some garden space along one edge of the house and none on the other.

Whether you are concerned about your tiny side garden or your seemingly nonexistent back garden, this book will help you find space where you think there is none and help you decide what to do with it. There is a chapter for each specific area of the garden, including the even more defined spaces on decks, patios, balconies, and rooftops. Each chapter identifies the difficulties inherent in that particular kind of space and offers solutions, so that no one will need to walk away with only one formula for the generic small garden. It's your garden, and your taste; this book will help you solve the problems so that you can get on with enjoying your garden.

At the back of the book are plant lists that supplement the plants already discussed in the chapters. The ten lists are organized to make it easy for you: trees, shrubs, ground covers, perennials, vines, narrow plants, hedge plants, ornamental grasses, variegated plants, and an underused group well suited to the small garden—small conifers. Each plant's listing not only gives you details on its cultural requirements and its best characteristics (fragrance, long season of bloom, striking fall color, and the like) but also alerts you to any problems associated with it (although the point is, for the most part, to avoid problem plants).

It's important for readers who do have small gardens to know that there are no smoke and mirrors in this book. The photographs that accompany the text were all taken in the Northwest, in truly small gardens, not just tiny corners of large ones. (I certainly would feel cheated if I knew that what was being held up to me as an example of what to do in a small garden was not small at all.) Anyone can have a good-looking corner when there's another acre behind it to stuff with plants; it's what you can do when you have only a 20-by-20-foot plot to plant that really matters.

Although the frustrations of limited space are not exclusive to the city, the majority of small gardens are in urban areas. Cities are increasingly "packing them in," building up population density to preserve actual open green spaces that play a greater role for wildlife habitat and pollution control. The result is that we have smaller lots in which to live and garden. All parts of the garden shrink—and sometimes the front, side, or back garden completely disappears.

Amid these frustrations, we strive to create our own green space, a private park. Some may think that because a garden is small, it must be sparsely planted and tightly designed in a clean, modern fashion. So untrue. Small gardens reflect what the gardener wants, just as larger ones do. Our gardens can be sleek or wild, modern or romantic. What they do need to be is year-round, because we see them every day of the year when we look out the kitchen window or walk to the car. Small gardens have nowhere to hide. So, let's make them—all parts of them—what we want them to be.

Chapter One

- ■ **Small-Garden Design Tips**

- ■ **Plant Selection for the Small Garden**

- ■ **Soil in the Small Garden**

- ■ **Here Comes the Sun**

- ■ **Watering the Small Garden**

- ■ **Replacing Grass with a Small Garden**

- ■ **Small Gardens and Urban Weather**

Left: **This house takes up most of the lot, leaving a small garden around the fringe. The picket fence and billowing plants such as the purple wallflower** *Erysimum* **'Bowles Mauve' soften the abrupt vertical lines of the house.**

Considerations

Small gardens need the same considerations as large gardens—attention to design, plant selection, soil, sun, and water. It's just that in the small garden these considerations are distilled into their essence—into an area that may not be much bigger than what, in a larger garden, might be used for the compost bin and the potting bench. In a compact garden, there are more extremes—too much, too little, too dry, too wet—and there is little room for the middle ground.

Microclimates are small areas that have different weather conditions from those prevailing in the area. The Northwest is noted for its weather "convergence zones," a phrase that Northwesterners take to mean that it could snow 3 inches five blocks away, while their gardens are merely damp. Microclimates also can occur within a neighbor-hood, such as on the west side of a hill or at the bottom of a slope, and they can even occur within a garden. A pocket of warmth next to the dryer vent and a south-facing wall offers the gardener the chance to grow plants that may be considered slightly out of range for the area. Hardscapes—walls, houses, fences, pavement—help create microclimates in a small garden that can actually extend and expand a gardener's palette of plants and styles; but in the high-rise city they can also create drying winds that whip down streets in a wind-tunnel effect. Too harsh an environment for a garden? Not at all; use these conditions to your advantage with proper plant selection.

Attention to details such as these, not restrictions to a particular style, are the keys to a successful small garden. A small garden doesn't have to be strictly formal or use only miniature plants. Instead, focusing on the vital components that make up a fabulous garden—whether it be wild, formal, modern, or Victorian—can make a garden that will "work" for you. Observing, visiting, and drawing on the accumulated ideas and techniques of other gardens and gardeners can be a satisfying way of creating your own space. You pick and choose what you want in a variety of designs, and even if you turn over the framework design to a professional, you can still be in charge of filling in all the blanks.

Small-Garden Design Tips

Our small gardens are typically framed by walls and fences, utility poles and sidewalks. In a large garden you can impose your own series of elaborate garden rooms on the landscape, but in a small garden the areas already tend to be well defined: front, side, and back. Furthermore, we find that some of our precious garden space must be used to accommodate and disguise elements of modern life—the trash can, recycling bins, neighbors. There is no "back 40" in which to hide them. Sometimes, there isn't even a driveway or a garage.

Garden space is the first consideration of design. In a small garden, or on a balcony or patio, the limits are often already fixed—right here is the front door, and 10 feet away, there is the sidewalk; here there is room for a table, a chair, and a few pots, and just beyond that is a crosswalk on a busy street corner. No matter how many beautifully drawn plans you look at, the neighbor's bedroom window will not move. So, instead of searching for the already-completed drawing that will fit your garden, use some basic design techniques when and where they work for you.

■ **Lay a path that will enhance and enlarge, not compress, your small garden.** As lovely as winding paths are on large estates, in the small garden the deliberately curved path often turns into a switchback trail, a squiggly line with no purpose. A gentle curve works better and looks less cluttered, and if there is a noticeable reason for the path to bend—to go around a tree, for example—it makes more sense.

Below: **The gentle curve of this front path was designed to skirt the thickly layered planting. Curved paths make sense when, as here, there is a reason for the path to bend.**

■ **Soften straight lines with billowing plants, well-placed containers, and other devices.** The 90-degree angles of a space will visually bend to the expression of the gardener's style. In fact, blurring the hard boundaries (fences, walls) of a garden with vines or with groups of plants gives the effect of more space, not less, by giving the impression that the garden doesn't end there.

■ **Use color to change the size of the garden.** The use of color can help the garden appear larger or smaller than it is. Red, purple, and white are colors that advance; a pot of red geraniums planted at the back corner will visually shorten the 20-foot distance and make that corner appear much closer. Pastels at a distance, though, create a sense of depth, a feeling that the garden extends farther than its edges. This technique works well when you see the garden from one entrance only. It can backfire on you, however: if you enter the garden from the back gate, the pot of red geraniums on the deck will immediately jump out at you.

■ **Divide the garden to make it seem larger.** Divide a square into four sections, and you end up with smaller spaces. But in a small garden, divisions can make the garden seem more spacious, because there's always another place to sit, another view to take in. This technique works well when you want to use different styles; you can have a small herb garden, a Japanese-style pond, and a woodland garden too. It's the same concept as the creation of "garden rooms" within a large garden, where several different spaces (each one probably as big as your entire back garden) are separated by hedges or hardscapes and differentiated by theme plantings. In the small garden, if you tried to wall off many tiny areas, you'd end up with closets, not rooms. But you can create a feeling of different areas in the small garden by using the conditions that exist: the herb garden goes in the sunniest spot, and the woodland garden, even though it's within full view, is appropriately placed under the shade of a few tall trees.

■ **Use hedges only around the perimeter.** Along the edge of a small garden, a high wall or hedge can create privacy; within the small garden, it can get claustrophobic.

■ Within the garden, create divisions using "see-through" and "see-over" methods:

● Keep walls low and hedges short enough to see over. A low hedge of lavender in the sun, or of Japanese holly *(Ilex crenata)* in part shade, gives the feeling of division without cutting up the garden into tiny pieces.

● Walking through an arbor gives the impression of moving into a separate space, without the closed-in feel that a looming hedge gives. Cover the arbor in vines or climbing roses—it's one more place to grow something.

● Openwork fences—pickets, or square or diamond-shaped lattices—and see-through bamboo screens give the illusion of separate spaces without boxing you in. And the spaces in an open fence are ideal for vines to grow through.

Above: **Picket fences are see-through barriers, giving the garden an open feel; they mix well with plants that, like this rose, can grow through them.**

■ **Change levels for a new perspective.** Walking up or down a few steps to a new level will alter your view and make you feel as if you're in a new, separate place. A deck that is even three steps up from the rest of the garden can expand the space in a small garden. It also gives you more planting room—you have space for containers in addition to the garden "below." If you have a flat garage roof, check to see how sturdy it is—it could be the perfect place for a hot Mediterranean garden. In the small garden, it's a valuable asset to be able to move such a short distance, perhaps as little as 10 feet, and experience an entirely new perspective.

■ **Borrow views and ideas.** It's a Japanese design technique to "borrow" the view of a distant mountain by framing it with trees or shrubs in one's own garden. The owner of a small American garden can use the same technique to good purpose; borrowing a view even a few houses away will open up the garden, making it feel larger than it is. What can you see from your garden? A particularly beautiful and large flowering cherry across the street? Can you see the city skyline from your deck? Use plants as you would the frame of a picture,

Above: **Steps divide the two levels of this garden, making the area seem more spacious. Planted in containers on the steps are summer annuals and tender perennials, including pelargoniums, with a potted angel's trumpet (Brugmansia) towering above them.**

placing taller plants on each side of the view. It's better to choose plants with a narrow growth habit so that your own "frame" won't eventually encroach on the view. Use a graduated planting in front of the main view, so that the eye naturally sweeps from the ground-level plants up toward the picture.

■ **Hide the boundaries to give yourself more room.** If you can't see where the gate or fence is—if it's hidden from view—then the garden doesn't seem to have an end. Use shrubs that are soft and billowing or narrow and upright to disguise the edges of the garden. A lattice trellis with a vine clambering over it will also do the trick in front of a gate.

Plant Selection for the Small Garden

The most important part of planning any small garden is plant selection, because it takes into consideration all aspects of your garden—climate, soil, site, and water. Gardeners with small plots need to be choosy about their plants. We don't have room for aggressive plants that want to hog all the space, nor can we put up with many failures, because they stick out like a sore thumb. Too often, the solution is to just stick in a couple of rhododendrons and a laurel hedge—isn't that the Northwest way?—and forget about it.

Selecting the Right Plants

Good plant selection can make the difference between a healthy garden and disaster. Here in the maritime climate of the Puget Sound region, one can still see old and sick specimens of blue spruce (*Picea pungens* 'Glauca'). It doesn't get cold enough here to kill off the woolly adelgid that attacks the needles, so most of these trees have branches that are bare almost to the tips. And Northwest gardeners are still making similar mistakes. In the planning of a new or renovated garden, plant selection is often relegated to second-class status. Most of us go to the nursery, fall in love with a plant, buy it, and then make excuses for its placement. And so we see shade-loving *Skimmia* planted in the sun (where its foliage, attacked by spider mite, becomes stippled), roses in the shade (suffering from powdery mildew), or a gorgeous but rampant *Clematis montana* overwhelming a spot better suited to a more petite member of the genus.

As much fun as random plant buying can be, it's deeply satisfying to know you have the right conditions for a plant. If possible, work in reverse order. Look first at the conditions of your garden, and *then* start your search: you want a small evergreen shrub, for part to full shade, that doesn't mind dry soil in the summer. Visit gardens and nurseries, ask questions, read books, look at plant lists (such as those at the back of this book). The plant you need is there.

Using This Book's "Plant Lists"

The ten plant lists at the back of this book will give you a multitude of ideas for your small garden. The plants listed are all fabulous, offering a range of characteristics and growth habits to satisfy any gardener with limited planting area (and even those with lots of space!). The lists are organized by type of plant (grasses, ground covers and edgers, hedges, narrow plants, perennials, shrubs, small conifers, trees, variegated plants, and vines and climbers), and they "tell it like it is," providing practical information about the plants' good characteristics as well as any potential problems.

You won't find the most common plants in these lists, and there are few repeats of plants described within the chapters (no sense wasting space—we know what that is like). Instead, these supplemental lists are filled with plants that are often labeled in horticulture books as "underused" and "should be more widely grown."

It won't take Sherlock Holmes to find these plants. First look at your local nursery, and, if you don't see what you want there, ask. Nursery staff want you to find the right plant as much as you want to have it, so ask whether they can order it for you, or if some will be coming in with an order. Some nurseries are so customer-oriented that they will tell you the name of another, often specialty, nursery where you might be able to find what you want. You may be a catalog shopper, in which case you'll often find plants that won't be on the nursery tables.

Selecting for Size

Size counts. If you have a narrow walkway—say 3 feet of planting space and a 2-foot-wide path around the side of your house—there is little point in planting a *Ceanothus* 'Julia Phelps'; its bulk will take up at least every inch of that 5-foot width, if not more. Your constant chore will be to keep the shrub "under control"—a euphemism for repeatedly cutting it back until the structure and natural shape of the plant is long gone. In addition, such inappropriate care will likely weaken it, inviting pests and diseases to move in. And that path is probably too shady for a *Ceanothus* anyway—and a good plant in the wrong place is another invitation to pest and disease problems. Put that *Ceanothus* in the front or back corner of the garden, and it can spread its 5 feet without getting in anyone's way. You can enjoy the butterflies its deep blue flowers will attract each spring, without being menaced by the swarms of bees it will also draw.

Don't think you always have to choose dwarf plants. Take a second look at whatever trees you have. Older small gardens often come equipped with large trees. Good structure is hard (and slow) to come

Above: **This summer-flowering small tree, *Eucryphia* x *nymansensis*, is a perfect choice for a narrow spot because it grows up to about 20 feet but spreads to only 8 feet.**

by, so don't be too quick to take them all out just to get some sunshine. Be selective and, with the help of a certified arborist, decide which are the healthiest trees. Established trees can be limbed up, conifers can be thinned, and suddenly you have a shady place to sit and the makings of a woodland garden.

In the small garden, size does matter. However, it is impossible to tell to the inch how big a plant will grow, so put the tape measure away. So many factors influence eventual size—sun, soil, water, location—that plants are almost like snowflakes: no two are the same. As disconcerting as this may be when you are investing time, money, and, most important, space in woody plants, it would be irresponsible to say that a particular tree will grow to 10 feet tall, because as soon as that information is in print, some exacting gardener would be out there with a tape measure to prove that, in fact, it will grow to 10 feet and 3 inches.

Instead of expecting a to-the-inch height and width, think of the sizes given in the "Trees" list at the back of this book as general guidelines. "Small" trees are generally considered those that grow to about 30 feet, unless stated otherwise. The list also tells you their growth habit; a "broadly spreading" tree is not one to put in the 10-foot space between the house and the fence. Where width is limited, use the "Narrow Plants" list.

Creating Multiseason Interest

Choose plants that do more than one thing. There is a way to have the best for your small garden—even if you can't have it all—with seasonal changes of flowers, foliage, bark, and bud. Plan with some conscious effort, and you will end up with more plants that have multi-season interest and fewer that are unchanging backdrops. Shade-tolerant longleaf mahonia *(Mahonia nervosa)* has early-spring flowers, summer berries, and winter foliage in shades of claret. Three seasons for one plant! Even conifers serve more than one purpose: in winter they add some green and life to the landscape; in spring, summer, and fall they act as a backdrop for the parade of color.

Soil in the Small Garden

We all yearn for soil with a light, fluffy texture, well drained, with lots of organic matter, and a neutral pH except for, perhaps, a pocket or two of slightly acid soil for those members of the heather family. In the small garden, the reality can be far from the ideal. In addition, soil types in the Northwest are directly linked to the last glacier, which was here a mere 10,000 years ago. The contours of the land—ridges and valleys—were formed by the glacier as it made its way south and then retreated. In its wake, it left heavy clay in valleys, making them prone to flooding, and patches of gravelly, rocky soil almost everywhere.

Below: **Whenever possible, choose plants that have more than one season of interest. Here, a coralbark maple (*Acer palmatum* 'Sango Kaku') displays its winter stem color.**

Chemicals in the Small Garden

Going organic has never looked so good. In the small garden, we are excruciatingly close to our plants—not just to what they put out in the way of pollen, sap, fruit, and fragrance, but to what we put on them. Reducing or eliminating the use of chemicals in the garden makes sense not only for peace of mind but for ease of gardening. Integrated Pest Management (IPM) is a process wherein chemical controls for pests and diseases are the very last to be used, and then only in a specific, confined, and controlled manner. Organic gardening practices use no synthetic chemicals for fertilizer or pest and disease control. In both IPM and organic gardening, choosing the right plant for the right place is of utmost importance. Plant pathologists, extension agents, and experts at your local nursery will all tell you that the vast majority of plant problems are due to cultural causes that include not only a plant in the wrong place, but a plant that has been improperly pruned or overwatered. A stressed plant is a blinking neon sign to pests and disease: "Eat Here!"

Maintaining an organic small garden means never having to say "Don't touch that plant, I just sprayed it." You don't have to take up valuable space to store opened and little-used bottles and boxes of chemicals, or carry the leftovers to special toxic-waste disposal stations. You use no broad-spectrum pesticides that kill off the good guys along with the (real or imagined) bad. Your small garden will be one where, on your way to the front door, you can pick a few pansies to sprinkle on your salad. (For more information, see "Can I Go Organic in My Small Garden?" in Chapter Seven.)

Understanding Soil

Soil needs to be a living, breathing organism whether it's in a small garden or in a container. Soil is made up of particles of minerals that have been chipped, cracked, and sloughed off rocks over time. The particles come in three sizes—sand particles are largest, next silt, and then clay—and the percentage of each gives the soil its texture. The other ingredient in soil (although, typically, this is at only about 5 percent of total volume) is humus, or organic matter (the decayed remains of leaves, twigs, insects, and other flora and fauna). Understanding the makeup of the different soil types in your small garden will help you grow healthier plants.

Soil texture is described according to the varying proportions of the particle sizes; a soil of mixed sizes is called a loam; and so there are sandy loams, where sand is the highest proportion, clayey loams, which are highest in clay, and silty loams, where silt is most abundant. A soil of all sand or even a sandy loam has large (relatively speaking) air pores between particles. With sand as the largest proportion, your soil is guaranteed to have good drainage—and keeping roots free of standing water is necessary for plant health (except for those bog-loving plants, such as *Rodgersia*). It's also guaranteed that during dry spells you will have to water any plants that are not accustomed to such arid conditions.

The presence of the smaller particles of silt and clay keeps a soil from going bone-dry quickly, because these smaller particles trap and keep water between them better than sand. Ideally, a soil's ingredients, in descending proportions, would be sand, silt, and clay.

Common Soil Problems

The soil in a small garden is often compacted, over-worked, or gone altogether. It's very likely that the soil structure—the way the particles are held together—has been broken down from construction or compaction. In all but the sandiest of soils, foot traffic can also break it down. Soil structure can make a huge difference in how your plants fare. Compacted soil acts like waterlogged soil, because the air pores, so vital to roots and soil fauna, are missing.

It could be that your small garden is long established, with soil so filled with tree and shrub roots that planting anything else seems impossible. The ground may be hard to penetrate, and of poor nutrition. Or you might have a new garden—a clean slate—one where the house or condominium was recently built. That means that the topsoil was scraped off and hauled away or stockpiled somewhere. Heavy construction vehicles have driven over and parked on what was left, compacting the soil and making it difficult for roots to breathe and water to drain.

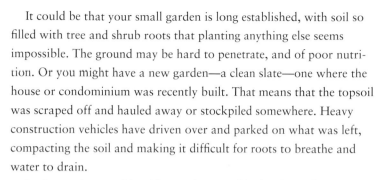

Below: **Soil in the small garden is often over-worked and compacted, but, as is evident here, regular applications of organic matter (compost, composted manure) improve soil conditions for plants.**

In city gardens, and in older gardens outside the city, soil can contain some surprises. At the end of a construction job, workers—obviously not gardeners themselves—often bury leftover materials. Pieces of concrete, the last scrapings from the bucket, trimmings from rebar, wood—you name it, and it's been found buried in the garden. Remnants of previous "civilizations" are also present. I found bricks in my community vegetable garden (artifacts of an old trolley station) and iron spikes in the herb bed at home (from who knows what).

In the soil of the small garden, there's no room for the flotsam and jetsam of life. As fun as it may be to find pieces of past lives, this rubble displaces real soil. If, unbeknownst to you, there is a cache of construction rubble next to the one new tree you decided you had room for in your small plot, that tree's roots will grow into the soilless pocket. The large air spaces between the pieces of rubble can fill with water, at best killing those roots, and at worst becoming a haven for soil-borne pathogens such as root rot. If the water does drain, the roots are left high and dry

to die. One of the functions of roots, plant stability, is lost, too; without a good anchor in the soil the tree can be thrown in the wind.

Finally, even small gardens can have a variety of soil textures throughout. We all complain about pockets of heavy soil, soil full of rocks (which seem to regenerate), or soil that dries out before we've finished watering. Just because a garden is small doesn't mean you can't have a pocket of clay in back and gravelly sand out front. (Here is another example where plant selection saves the day: choosing a plant well suited to clay and to part shade—say, the classic small boxwood *Buxus sempervirens* 'Suffruticosa'—can avoid problems from the beginning.)

You can make a difference with either of the two extremes—sandy soil and heavy, clayey soil—by adding well-composted organic matter as a yearly mulch (see "Organic Mulches" below). And the rocks? Gather them up (by the bucketful, I'm sure) and use them in areas where you want to keep the mud down, such as around the trash or at the base of a bird feeder, or under containers to help with drainage. You could even make your own small dry streambed feature.

Raised Beds

Left: **Raised beds solve problems in the small garden. They are a way to avoid poor soil, and they prevent feet from stomping on plants. Here, a raised bed lined with brick that matches the path creates a hospitable garden for daylilies (*Hemerocallis* cultivars), *Astilbe*, yarrow (*Achillea*), and petunias.**

To avoid problems, especially in poorly draining clay soils, you can build up. Even small gardens can accommodate raised beds of one kind or another. You can be creative with the shape of the bed—a circle, a square, a kidney shape—or be more practical and build to fit the space. A berm at least 18 inches high will have enough depth for the roots of shrubs and small trees, and small vegetable patches are especially easy to confine to raised areas. Slope the soil down gradually at the sides for a contoured look.

Containers are the easiest "raised beds"; place a large container or a collection of pots on gravel at the very spot that doesn't drain well. Use a good topsoil and add more organic matter to it. Then, remember that your new garden bed—whether on the ground or contained—will dry out faster than flat ground. Either remember to water more often in dry spells or select plants that can tolerate arid soil.

Organic Mulches

In an effort to neaten up a small garden's appearance and create a weed-suppressing top coat for the soil, many gardeners look to inorganic mulches such as lava rocks or black plastic. Even some organic mulches, including the jumbo-sized bark nuggets, can look and act inorganic. These materials may act as a (temporary) shield (until some weed seeds blow in and land on top of the covering), but they do little to enrich the soil. Some mulches can even go so far as to create abiotic conditions, meaning that the soil underneath cannot breathe and thus becomes a harbor for root rot and other soil-borne diseases.

Using an organic mulch in the small garden does double duty: suppressing weeds and enriching the soil. Organic matter is as good a weed-suppressant as any lava rock. It also enriches the soil, because worms and other beneficial creatures come up to the soil surface and take the humus back down with them. It can prevent soil erosion, reducing compaction and runoff, and it decreases the need for water during dry spells. All this, and it still gives a lovely, rich-looking dressing to the garden. A good-looking organic mulch is an easy yet vital part of a small garden, where every inch counts. Here are some good ones:

■ Well-composted yard waste.

■ Well-composted dairy or chicken manure (often composted with wood chips or shredded bark and leaves).

■ Sewer sludge, also called biosolids. (Class A biosolids are free of disease pathogens, but even so, many gardeners prefer to use this product in the ornamental garden only.)

■ Wood chips and shredded/chipped material, which includes branches, stems, and leaves.

■ Bark. In the Northwest, this is usually the bark of Douglas fir. Available shredded or in chunks of graded sizes, bark is overused in the landscape and not attractive. Shredded bark lends a burnt-sienna tone to the garden, and the jumbo chunks are so useless that you might as well use hunks of plastic.

In the established small garden, full of a variety of woody plants and herbaceous perennials, you can apply organic mulch yearly. Winter is the easiest time to do this because you'll be able to see where you're putting it. Bulbs and most herbaceous perennials don't mind being covered with 2 or 3 inches of compost (there are exceptions—don't cover astilbes or hellebores). For shrubs, apply the mulch up to 6 inches or so from the trunk; keep it up to 12 inches away from tree trunks. Any mulch—compost, bark, or lava rock—pushed up against trees and shrubs creates a haven for disease and pests. A woody plant has trunk cells that are different from root cells; root cells are made to be underground, trunk cells are not.

Below: **Matching plants to sun exposure means fewer problems with pests and diseases. Happy in the sun here is a container of Mexican feather grass** *(Stipa tenuissima)* **with myrtle euphorbia** *(Euphorbia myrsinites)* **at its base**.

Here Comes the Sun

The amount of sunshine in the garden is variable, of course; it depends on the time of day and the season. It's also variable because many of us pretend that our gardens get more sun than they really do. Although some plants may be accommodating as far as the amount of sun they need, others are more particular. So, to help you choose plants for your garden, here are the terms for the different amounts of sun, and what they mean:

■ **"Full sun" means at least six hours of direct sunlight a day on the plant.** And that's out of a fourteen-hour summer day. The extreme example would be any area of the garden that gets full sun plus reflected light (and radiated heat) from buildings or other hard surfaces. The gardener who has such a spot can use it selectively to provide space for plants that may be borderline hardy in her region. Flannel bush *(Fremontodendron californicum),* with deep yellow 2-inch flowers in summer, is inconsistently hardy to Zone 8, but can grow here in full sun with its back against the wall.

■ **"Part sun" or "part shade" means about four to six hours of sun a day.** The two terms are interchangeable (although in some places you'll read that the first indicates more sun than the second), so choosing "part sun" over "part shade" doesn't make you an optimist. Often it's important to note whether the shade is in the morning or the afternoon; for example, some plants prefer protection from the hot afternoon sun, and roses need morning sun to dry off their foliage.

■ **"Light shade" is usually dappled shade from deciduous trees.** As the sun travels across the sky, it hits the leaves of understory plants in little patches, changing as the day goes on. This provides the much-needed sun for photosynthesis. Notice that plants that do well in part shade usually have larger leaves (for more hits of sun) and thinner leaves (so that unabsorbed sun rays can pass through the top leaf and hit a lower one). Their leaves are more likely to be held horizontally on the plant (again, to catch the rays).

■ **"Deep shade" comes from dense trees, often conifers, especially those with limbs low on the trunk.** Even early-morning or late-afternoon rays can be blocked. Plants that do well in deep shade are usually understory plants in the wild—those that grow on the forest floor. Ferns come to mind immediately. In thick deciduous forests, many spring-blooming perennials take advantage of the winter sun that gets through the covering of bare branches. The rest of the year it may be quite dark for them.

■ **To this, we add another category of shade that we'll call "really most sincerely shade."** It's especially familiar to those with gardens on balconies or in other places where buildings, not plants, block the sun. Even in deep shade under trees, some sunlight may penetrate between leaves and branches, and sometimes even through thin leaves, without being captured for use in photosynthesis. But when the sun is blocked by a building—your house or the neighbor's—it can't penetrate, bounce off, or turn corners.

Sunlight changes in character as the year progresses, so it changes the character of our gardens. In the small garden, of course, the lower the sun is in the sky the more sunlight may be blocked, but even when the sun does appear, the light looks different at different times of the year.

As the sun's rays pass through our atmosphere, they are scattered by air molecules and particles of dust. At midday in summer, the light rays have a fairly direct and clear path through the atmosphere. When the sun is low in the sky—at sunrise, at sunset, and during the winter—its rays pass through more atmosphere, and therefore more "stuff." This is especially true in the Northwest, where the sun spends much of the winter barely (it seems) above the horizon. Blue wavelength is the most easily scattered, so it is most often lost at these times, leaving red wavelengths, which produce a redder—although not necessarily warmer—light in our gardens. You've experienced it yourself: when September comes, even though the temperatures may be warm, there is a perceptible change in the quality of light and in the appearance of our gardens—they seem to glow.

Below: **Deep shady corners of the small garden can be brightened with plants such as variegated Solomon's seal (*Polygonatum odoratum* 'Variegatum') and sunny yellow Welsh poppy (*Meconopsis cambrica*).**

How to Follow the Sun

Track the sun in your small garden, and you'll know at what point it will break through between the neighbor's house and the large Douglas fir across the alley. You'll be able to tell if the place where you want to plant an herb garden really does get full sun.

The farthest north that the sun is ever directly overhead is along the Tropic of Cancer, 23.5 degrees north of the equator. This happens on the summer solstice (June 21), the longest day of the year. As you move north of that latitude, the sun is less than directly overhead on June 21. In the Pacific Northwest, we live anywhere from about 21 (Eugene) to 26 (Vancouver, B.C.) degrees north of the Tropic of Cancer. That means that, for us, on the longest day of the year, the sun is that many degrees from overhead.

Here's how to use this information to track the sun in your own garden:

■ Face south and hold your arm straight overhead, forming a 90-degree angle with the earth.

■ Lower your arm about 24 degrees (depending on where you live) to find the highest point of the sun (your personal summer solstice).

■ Now, point your arm toward the eastern horizon, and move it in an arc across the sky to the sunset in the west, being sure to keep the summit at your own summer solstice.

You will be approximating the path of the sun through your garden. Did you know that the hemlock two doors down was tall enough to block the sun at 2 in the afternoon?

Made in the Shade

Shade plays a big part in the small garden, and its effects on plants that need sun are obvious. They produce elongated, weak stems that bend toward whatever light is available; they also produce fewer leaves, with longer lengths of stem between them (the part of the stem between sets of leaves is called the internode). This phenomenon is called etiolation, and is triggered when a plant doesn't get the light it needs. Hormones are released that cause the more shaded side of a stem to grow cells that are longer than on the side where light hits it. This helps the plant turn toward and capture whatever light is available. The plant uses up a lot of energy on this growth, and it usually isn't worth it—the plant expends more energy than it can take in. Like any plant in an inappropriate place, these plants are more susceptible to pests and diseases because of their weakened state. Plants that grow stocky and robust in full sun look weak and spindly in shade.

Plants that need shade but somehow get pushed onto the full-sun scene have their own set of problems. Leaves of plants that are adapted to shade typically grow broad and thin so that a maximum number of cells is available to catch sun for photosynthesis. Such plants, if grown in full sun, can get burned or bleached out and, again, will be more susceptible to pests and diseases.

Watering the Small Garden

We've all done it at one time or another, and, probably, we're still doing it under the pressure of "Where will I put this plant?" in a garden with limited space. In our shade gardens we've planted a moisture-loving *Astilbe* side by side with Mrs. Robb's spurge (*Euphorbia amygdaloides* var. *robbiae*), a fine small evergreen shrub for dry soils.

Down the way there's a *Rodgersia*, needing water to look its best, next to a clump of Pacific Coast iris that doesn't want to see the hose in August, if you don't mind.

Grouping Like-Minded Plants

Watering the garden can be quite a conundrum—there are so many plants, and a finite number of places for them. The ideal would be to

group all of our plants according to their water needs, also remembering soil and sun requirements. The reality is that we have a limited amount of space and there are some plants that are just too fabulous to pass up.

Our weather in the Northwest is referred to as a cool Mediterranean climate. That means that our rain falls mostly from October through April. July, August, and often September have little measurable rainfall. This fact should be uppermost in your mind

Above: **Grouping plants by water needs reduces water use and your work time. Here, a moisture-loving lacecap hydrangea and gooseneck loosestrife (Lysimachia clethroides) keep company.**

when grouping plants. Combine plants that don't need summer water with plants that can live without summer water and still look decent (there's a difference), and plant moisture-loving plants with those that tolerate water provided they are in well-drained soil. Sometimes fiddling with the amount of sun can help: Bishop's hat (*Epimedium* spp.) prefers moist soil, but as long as it's in shade, the plant may get along fine with less water than you'd expect. This kind of experiment is one that many gardeners don't want to conduct, especially if it is on display for all to see, but if you're willing to take a chance, you may get delightful results.

Watering Systems and Methods

What kinds of water systems work in the small garden? Here's a huge benefit of having a small garden: you don't have as much area to water or as far to drag the hose. Whether you hand-water, keeping a close eye on how much water goes where, or prefer to have a timed system, you have more choices than carrying around a watering can.

■ **Dragging the hose around:** Some gardeners plant so that they can water by hand as far as the hose will reach, and everything else is on its own. They choose their plants to match this watering system.

■ **Using a coiled hose for limited distances:** These "hoses" popped on the scene a few years ago; they come in lengths up to 50 feet. They look like long telephone cords, and, like telephone cords, they can become twisted (despite what the advertising says). However, they might be just the ticket for hand-watering a balcony or deck.

■ **Soaker hoses:** These rough, black hoses are usually made from recycled tires. They are perforated so that they're leaky. Snake them through beds before you lay mulch down (billowing foliage and flowers usually do a good job of camouflage), and then connect one end to a hose that goes to the faucet. You can turn the hose on and off or set a timer at the faucet. Soaker hoses are a low-tech, low-cost watering system. The water leaking through slowly penetrates the soil (spreading up to 2 feet across, depending on the soil type). You leave the water on for a couple of hours, which seems like a long time, but you only have to water once a week or less.

■ **Emitter irrigation:** Thin black coils are extended from plant to plant or container to container in this system. At each plant or container, an emitter is attached that, when the water is turned on, drips or sprays water. Good for decks, these are a hassle in garden beds.

■ **Underground sprinkler systems:** The best time to install an underground system, even in the small garden, is before the garden is installed. Otherwise, you'll be digging up patio pavement and decks to get it all going.

Keep an eye on timed systems. Timed watering systems may seem extravagant in the small garden, but they can be useful for areas that need supplemental water when you may be on vacation. Too often, however, they are a waste of not only water but money. The timing is set by computer, and you are in charge of changing the settings, so there shouldn't be an excuse for the sprinklers turning on in the rain or watering the sidewalk and people passing by, or—and this is where it really hits home for gardeners—letting some heads clog up, so that the precious rhododendron that should be getting water is getting nothing. If you invest in an automatic system, be it drip or sprinkler, test it occasionally by looking at all the heads when the water is on to make sure they are working and hitting the right part of the garden.

Replacing Grass with a Small Garden

Here's an amazing thing about grass. When you have it, you work like the devil to keep it looking decent. It's always dying off in spots; moss tries to take over; there are weeds everywhere; you have to water and cut it constantly. But just try getting rid of it and planting something else. Suddenly, you have a lovely crop of grass coming up in all the places you don't want it, grass that never looked that good when you tried to tend it.

A small garden doesn't need to be totally without a patch of grass. Most gardeners prefer to have some lawn to set off the flowers, trees, and shrubs. And if you lack a deck, you need some lawn for the chaise longue.

But some sections of lawn just aren't worth the trouble. Grass in the planting strip next to the street, grass on a slope, or those long, thin strips of grass near a border (where you'd much rather have just a little more room for plants) can become too annoying to mess with.

Once you have determined to remove sod, the first thing to decide is whether you're in a big hurry. There are quick methods of removing sod, and there are slower ones. The quick ways require hard work, but you can plant sooner than with the slow ways, which require very little work; for these you have to wait up to a year to do anything with the spot. How impatient are you? Following are various ways you can remove grass.

Digging Up and Reusing Sod

Dig up sod with a sod cutter or shovel. Sod cutters are big machines, not suitable for small areas or places confined by barriers such as trees and fences. (The sod beneath a tree would be too shallow to use a mechanical cutter on anyway; you'd end up damaging tree roots, most of which are in the top 18 inches of soil.) They are easier to use on a planting strip, but they are unwieldy no matter where you are (unless you really like big machines). Digging up sod shovelful by shovelful requires that you not get carried away with how deep the shovel is going. The roots of grass aren't more than about 3 inches deep, and there's no sense in taking a lot of excess soil with you—it's heavy enough work as it is. Shake the hunks of sod to remove as much of the soil as possible, but don't wear yourself out; grass has a fine root structure and holds more soil than it's willing to give up.

Once the grass is cut or dug, you now have piles and piles of unwanted sod. Where will you put it? This is where the gardener with a small space gets really inventive. The ideal thing would be to compost the sod, creating a new pile that you can cover with black plastic. The covering is important because, even when you turn the pieces upside down, grass has a sneaky way of turning itself around and continuing to grow. Composting sod this way can take up to a year, at which time you can break up the pieces and mix them with your compost pile. You will have some lovely humus for the garden.

Piles of sod can be useful. If you have only one pile of sod, or if you are creating a berm and can use the hunks (turned upside down) as the lower level and cover them with several inches of clean soil or compost, you can get away with keeping all of it. Or ask around; you may be able to give it away to other gardeners who need it for the same purposes. A load halved is a load lightened—just think what turning it into eighths would do.

Smothering the Grass

Get rid of grass slowly. Leaving the grass in place but smothering it by excluding air and water will kill it off over time (at least six months, but a year is safer). The benefit of this is that you don't have piles of sod to deal with; once dead, the grass quietly composts in place, adding organic matter to the soil. But even when you use this technique, you will need to cut a border of sod off from around the perimeter. This ensures that all the grass will be covered, because if any is left to peek out the edges, it will live.

Use sheets of heavy black plastic, well anchored with bricks or rocks. This method will slowly kill off the grass, although you'll need to wait for what seems like an eternity. Cover the grass in August, and you may be able to uncover and plant in May. You might be able to steel yourself to look at this scene for a year, but in a small garden where it may be all you have to look at, that's unlikely. If you can stand it, when it's "finished" you can dig, loosen the soil, and plant.

You can also cover the grass with cardboard or several layers of newspaper, topped with two or three inches of compost. It will still take a year to kill the grass, but the cardboard or newspapers will decompose and add yet more humus to the garden. The earthworms and other assistants in decomposition will be busy the whole year the grass is covered.

Getting rid of sod in any of these ways will not ensure that you will have no grass coming back up, nor that you'll also be getting rid of all weeds—not even using chemicals to kill all of it will do that. Weed seeds buried a few inches down get turned up to the light and germinate. Seeds of grass and weeds get blown in from around the neighborhood. Weeds are too tenacious and too easily adapted to harsh conditions to be dispatched easily. Their motto is "Grow fast, live hard, die young."

Below: **When replacing a lawn with a garden, completely kill off or remove sod before planting, and use an organic mulch to help make maintenance easier.**

Small Gardens and Urban Weather

Contradictions in the city are rife: everyone wants public transportation, yet we refuse to get out of our cars; rents are high, yet there are
no vacancies. Following on the heels of human nature in the city are
contradictions in climate: how can humidity be lower yet precipitation
higher? Moisture should be, after all, moisture, and if it falls from the
sky, why does it not hang around in the air longer?

Humidity—the amount of moisture in the air—is a result of several
factors: the amount of open water in an area (the sea, for example, or
a large lake or bay), the amount of rainfall, and the amount of moisture that evaporates from the ground.

Although coastal cities have nearby open water, many of the for-
merly open waters within cities are now underground, channeled into
storm drains. The streams and creeks that meandered through wooded
pockets on their way to larger rivers and eventually to the ocean have,
for the most part, been crowded out by office buildings, apartment
buildings, and our houses.

Small Gardens, Humidity, and Storm Drains

The rain falls on everyone, it's true, but when the rain falls in the
country, it doesn't all hit the ground at the same time. Instead, it is
intercepted by trees. Their leaves and needles gather a few drops at a
time. Some rain glides slowly down crevices in the bark. Water clings
to the leaves and flowers of plants, and the impact of rain on the
ground is softened and delayed. At ground level it is slowed again by
the layers of organic matter—decaying leaves, rotting stumps—uneven
surfaces that provide a natural mulch for the soil below.

In the city, the rain hits hard pavement. It falls on roofs and rushes
out downspouts. It gathers in the gutters and flows to storm drains,
where it is taken safely out of our way—unless there is too much
volume for the storm drains to handle. The decreased humidity in the
city is the result of less vegetation and open ground to intercept moisture and hold it long enough for it to evaporate into the air.

Open green spaces—even small gardens—can make a difference in
both the amount of run-off and the humidity in an urban area. After a

good soaking, trees, shrubs, and undergrowth glisten with moisture, and the organic layer and the soil below it are wet. The layers of plants and mulch in a small city garden act as a sponge, reducing the immediate flow of rain to the storm drains and helping to keep storm waters at bay. When the rain finishes, the moisture begins to evaporate into the air, increasing the humidity.

Small Gardens and Urban Temperatures

More green space also means more plants to transpire and thus more moisture to be released into the air. Walk into a park or under a group of trees on a hot, sunny day and feel the temperature difference. Compare that with walking under an awning. Trees cool not only by blocking the sun but also by transpiring—giving off moisture. Many of us grew up using swamp coolers in the summer. They work on the same principle as transpiration—air pulled through moisture is cooled (see the sidebar "Plant Transpiration"). The moisture lost to a plant can help cool the air around it, and studies have shown that this is a clear benefit to cities, because it helps alleviate urban heating. Even small gardens can do their part to keep cities cool: plant a tree in the small garden to cool off.

Small Gardens and Air Quality

Small gardens help reduce air pollution. It is now common in the summer to hear the daily weather report include pollution information, warning people who suffer from asthma or other breathing problems that they must monitor their activity level. And we have all seen the buildup of haze and clouds after several warm, sunny days. Normally, the earth (including the pavement and buildings of a city) is warmed by the sun during the day and then gives off that heat at night. Plants can help reduce pollution by capturing particulates (have you noticed how dusty plants can get after days without rain?) and, again, moderating the temperatures in built-up areas.

Plant Transpiration

Transpiration is a plant process that involves water, air temperature, and humidity. The water that is absorbed by a plant's root system is transported up through the plant's xylem—sort of like straws going up the main stem, out onto lateral stems, into twigs and leaves. The water that is used by each cell to keep plump and alive is also turned into vapor by the heat of the sun and is transpired—that is, released—by the plant through tiny openings in the leaves (usually on the underside) called stomata.

The pull of water up the xylem from roots to leaves is similar to what happens when you drink through a straw—the pressure draws the liquid up. When the day is hot and dry, the air uses the plant like a straw, sucking up more and more water. For example, depending on conditions, a water-loving birch tree may transpire from 200 to 1,000 gallons a day during the growing season! Obviously, there are situations when more moisture is lost than the plant can take up. In such stressful periods, the stomata will close to prevent wilting.

Wind adds an even drier touch to the cocktail. As stomata release moisture vapor, a small, moist, protective shield is formed, like a little leaf atmosphere, with water-vapor molecules swarming around the stomata. Wind can whisk that all away and dry up the moist layer—which means using up more moisture from the plant as water rushes up the xylem to the drying leaves.

By being aware of a plant's water use, the gardener can stay attuned to its needs according to where it is growing (exposed or protected), the temperature, and the wind, especially during dry periods.

Left: There's little space between sidewalk and front door in this garden, but it's still plenty of room for a mix of perennials, including goldenrod (Solidago), Crocosmia, and brick-red daylilies.

The Front Garden

Small front gardens magnify all the typical design challenges because tight boundaries push everything into full view. We're more self-conscious about the front garden—it's our presentation to the world, a chance to put our best face forward. (Or, for that matter, to hide from it behind a high hedge.) Small front gardens don't have the benefit of being seen from a distance, which can turn almost any messy flower and shrub border into a charming vision of color. People can see every inch of your front garden. How does it look?

Shallow front gardens seem to preclude any normal-sized plants. Rounded shrubs appear voluminous, and one or two can fill the entire landscape, making a small garden look even smaller. This is notoriously the problem with foundation shrubs, which for generations have been planted up against the front of many houses as a matter of course. An old rhododendron or two, plus an English laurel, crowd out the walkway, plunge the porch and entry into darkness, and leave us no room for the plants we'd rather have. Not only does it take courage to do something about overgrown foundation shrubs, it takes knowing what is the best course of action.

At the other extreme, a mincing collection of dwarf plants makes the garden look like a Disneyland landscape. A garden made up of dots of color, with no plants bigger than a foot or two, looks piecemeal. Yet it's quite possible to design a shallow front garden that will be in scale with its surroundings and still include trees and shrubs, along with perennials.

Porches and entries afford more garden space, and gardeners with small holdings are always looking for one more place to put a plant. Sometimes the porch is about the only garden there is in front, so every effort must be made to create a garden with pots on the porch, plants climbing up the posts, and steps lined with containers. Seize the opportunity.

Entries, often dark and recessed, seem an unlikely place for living plants, but even those areas can be defined and decorated. The planting design for an entry shouldn't try to mimic larger mansions and English estates where huge, old yews stand as identical exclamation points flanking the door. It's possible to arrange even asymmetrical plantings around an entry for a pleasing effect.

Many front gardens in hilly Pacific Northwest cities have slopes that either plunge straight down to the sidewalk or stop at a retaining wall that's typically 3 to 4 feet high at sidewalk level. Gardeners with grass-covered slopes can be seen tying ropes to their lawn mowers so that the grass can be cut without gardener and machine toppling over. This attempt to maintain good-looking turf in these areas is not only dangerous but also futile. The top of the slope inevitably looks skinned, while the bottom is lush green.

Gardeners who try landscaping a slope often find that the plants at the top die and the ones at the bottom drown. Yet the slope may be all there is to the small front garden, so it's worth it to take the time and think about what will look good, from what angle, and how to manage it all. There are plenty of good planting ideas for a garden on a slope—and several methods of changing its contour—that will make the front garden look good whether you see it from the porch or at eye level from the sidewalk.

A corner lot presents twice the problem in the small urban front garden; now the world peers in on two sides instead of one. Bus stops, parking, and traffic times two. Along heavily traveled streets, the corner front garden can turn into a thoroughfare, with pedestrians cutting across to save a few steps. Gardeners who prefer to create some privacy for themselves believe they must put up a barricade. And instead of presenting one face to the public, the corner garden has an identity crisis. Where is the "real" front? Should both sides look the same? If plants are well chosen and well placed, the corner garden can be just as well defined as if there were only one front.

Below: **Planting strips can mean more garden, less mowing. This small garden has a sunny curbside area planted with lavender,** *Sedum* **'Autumn Joy', and gray Russian sage (***Perovskia atriplicifolia***).**

Below: **The front garden is yours, but this street view offers fun for everyone, with old-fashioned fox-gloves, poppies, iris, and lilies, and wisteria blooms dripping off the roofline.**

As if mowing on a slope wasn't enough of a problem, many gardeners try to maintain the grassy strip of land between sidewalk and street—variously called the planting strip, parking strip, extension, and other names less acceptable in polite company. This is the piece of the garden that's farthest from the house and the hose, which usually means it looks lumpy, weedy, and—naturally in our dry Pacific Northwest summers—brown. And everyone sees it. Gardeners who despair at growing anything out there: take hope. There are plants and designs that accommodate the space, the soil, and the function of this roadside garden, whether you're longing for a tree-lined street or a Mediterranean landscape.

Niggling problems loom large in the small garden. You can't escape far enough to get away from the noise of the street and traffic, so many gardeners look for ways to put up soundproof barriers. And then there's drainage: what to do with the yearly 30 inches or so of rainfall that rushes down off the roof? In a large garden, plastic sleeves take the rain from the downspouts far off into the lawn somewhere. In the small garden, the water would be draining into your neighbor's living room if you tried that. Deal creatively with these problems, and you get more garden and less frustration.

A good start with the small front garden is to really look at it, from

all possible angles. Stand across the street, walk by from both directions, look down out of an upstairs window and out the front window, drive by slowly in the car. How you design and plant your small front garden depends on how you use it and how you most often view it. Do you want to sit in it? Do you merely walk through it on the way to the door? Does it sit high up off the sidewalk? Later on, repeated assessment will help you spot plants that need changing—and may even surprise you with effects you wanted but didn't know you had achieved.

The Shallow Front Garden

Our gardens say a lot about us, but sometimes the context can say more. The small garden is confined by space, but within those limits much can be done. The front garden, in particular, can be defined by its surroundings. A garden only 10 feet deep from sidewalk to front door can be a collection of plants that complements the house, the entire garden becoming an entryway. Some front gardens may be up a set of steps, so that passersby see the ground at eye level; is what they see the bare stems at the base of a stand of summer phlox *(Phlox paniculata)*? When changes in height are part of the topography of the neighborhood, you must work with the retaining wall, slope, or rockery.

As with any part of the garden, how you use or view the front garden, its aspect (that is, its orientation to the sun), and its existing framework all combine to give you the design and structure you need.

Plant Densely

A shallow front garden can be densely planted with perennials and small shrubs in graduated sizes up to the porch rail. If you have a porch, you're already provided with a place to sit and drink iced tea or to set the groceries down as you search for your keys. Plant the shallow front garden densely, and place stepping-stones and narrow paths that can be used for maintenance—to reach plants to prune, deadhead, or cut back, and to provide access around to the side.

Plant close together with shrubs and perennials, and a low fence as a border along the sidewalk. You can fill up the space with perennials, shrubs, and a small tree, working from lowest (the fence at the sidewalk) to highest (the foundation). A 3-foot-high picket fence is well suited to vines, and for a year-round display it's best to choose an evergreen one such as *Clematis armandii*. Or this may be just the place for the wisteria, as all its wild growth will be in easy reach for control, as opposed to high atop an arbor or running along the roofline.

On view to the world, or a private oasis? With even a small front garden you can affect how the world sees you, and what you see of the world. On a busy street, say, if there's a bus stop right outside, those

Below: **This shallow front garden is planted densely, even along the fence line, where fall asters carry the floral show long past midsummer.**

10 feet become an important device in privacy; the garden becomes the barrier if you use a tall narrow hedge or a fence decorated with vines. You want privacy, but not necessarily isolation, so it's polite to offer a good view even though you've put up a "wall."

Share Front-Stoop Gardens

Front-stoop gardens can be shared. As cities have built up density to create more and more livable spaces for people, row houses have been reinvented. These long sets of attached houses or condominiums are built with comfort and style in mind, and that includes making room for gardens. The gardens have a community feel, so that sitting on the steps on a summer evening invites neighbors to stop by and chat. Cooperative gardening can include benches, artwork, food gardening, and flowers; the work doesn't seem overwhelming, because everyone can contribute resources of time and money, instead of those burdens falling on one person alone. Each small front garden can use a few repeating plants—for example, one of the mounding, dissected Japanese maples in each plot—and repeating or harmonizing colors, so that there is a unified look to the block. There will still be plenty of room for individual plant choices.

Foundation Shrubs

Bulky mounds of shrubs—in the Northwest that usually means a rhododendron, a lily-of-the-valley shrub *(Pieris)*, and a camellia—up against a house seem to be a requirement for home landscaping, as are the vertical elements (usually some conifer or other) planted at the corners of the house. These ubiquitous plantings originated with the building of much larger houses—and gardens—than are common today. Architects felt that the sudden perpendicularity where house met terra firma was too shocking and needed to be softened. Foundation shrubs were said to "ground" the house to the earth, making an easier transition for the eye. Foundation plants may be traditional, and traditionally needed, but they are enormous space-hogs when plunked into the small garden. They not only ground the house, they engulf it.

Fortunately, you can do something about the mounds of shrubs you already have. Deal with existing foundation shrubs by turning a critical eye to their placement and overall contribution to the garden. Then you have the information to decide whether to remove or renovate. And if you are choosing new foundation plants, you'll know which ones will be best.

Evaluating Existing Shrubs

Are the foundation shrubs out of scale for your house? If you have trouble seeing the house for the shrubs, you may need to take action. Trees aren't usually as much of a problem as bulky shrubs because their bare trunks create some visual space. Even if a tree is close to (and taller than) the front of the house, the house doesn't seem over-

Below: **The star magnolia (Magnolia stellata) grows into an elegant shrub, often multistemmed, and is covered with white blossoms in early spring.**

taken. But shrubs are usually mounds of foliage, and some broadleaf evergreens, such as rhododendrons and *Pieris*, can grow 10 feet wide and as tall, taking up far too much valuable space in the small garden as well as throwing the whole picture out of balance.

There are no bad shrubs, only shrubs that are in the wrong place or not maintained well. Any of the typical Northwest broadleaf evergreen shrubs can be retained and pruned (following its natural form), and you will end up with an elegant foundation shrub for the small garden. The bark of an older *Pieris*, for example, can be a rich brown, the outer layers shredding in long strips. But if your small front garden has one of each—rhododendron, *Pieris*, camellia, English laurel—it is better to choose to keep one or two than all of them.

Choose to retain a shrub that has elegant trunk and branching structure. Part the foliage and look beneath for multiple trunks or stems, which, when limbed up, will provide an interesting form. Keep the shrub that will offer flowers that speak to you: the fragrant rhododendron by the front door may be a better choice than the camellia with earlier but scentless flowers. Which is more important to you? And above all, always choose a shrub with the fewest disease and insect problems; this will cut your maintenance time by a lot.

Removing Shrubs

Have they got you surrounded? You may choose to remove some (or all) of your foundation shrubs, giving some breathing room to the house and the other plants. The best way to decide whether you need to remove some of them is to look at the front garden as others see it. Stand across the street, walk up and down, and look. A desire for privacy is one thing, but if you can't see the windows from the street (or can't see out of them when you're inside), the shrubs are taking over. Taking a photo of the front garden is an even more objective way to see whether you have too many foundation shrubs or whether they are too big. Lay a piece of tracing paper over the photo (this is for those of us who are not artists) and sketch in the house and the shape of each shrub, but leave one or two out. You'll soon see what will lighten the look of the front. And when you take out the extra plants, you'll be amazed at how much more garden you have.

If you are loath to dig up a large shrub and toss it, you can give it away. Find a local plant society, post a notice at the library, or talk it up at the grocery store. You have a fine specimen of fragrant, pink-flowering rhododendron that has "outgrown" its place in your garden, and you will give it away (free!—what a bargain!) to anyone who will come and dig it out.

What if your shrubs were good choices to begin with but now have problems? Sun and shade patterns change over the years as empty lots are built on and small trees become big. If the foundation shrubs in your small front garden have problems with pests and diseases, it could be because the sun (or shade) they need is gone. Better to move the shrub than to try to talk your neighbor out of that second-story addition.

Pruning Shrubs

Once you have decided which shrubs to keep, judicious pruning will make them into graceful additions to the small front garden instead of blobs. Shrubs are best pruned after flowering, so that you don't cut off any flowers for the next year. There are many excellent books on pruning, but to get you started, here are a few general guidelines:

■ Prune with bypass loppers or a small hand-pruning saw (not a chainsaw), removing branches back to another, larger branch.

■ Do not make a flush cut. Leave the "branch collar," the slight bulge where a branch meets a main trunk. Never make a heading cut (a random cut that leaves a stub). The stub is ugly enough, but with rhododendrons and many other shrubs, you'll get what's known as the "hydra effect"; buds all around the edge of the cut will sprout, making more of a mess than you started with. These stems will grow into a tangle of branches with weak wood that will break easily with wet snow or in the wind.

■ Take out one branch at a time, and check your work. Going slowly means you will be much less likely to say "Oops, that looks awful."

■ Never shear foundation shrubs such as rhododendron, forsythia, camellia, *Pieris,* and lilac. You'll end up with gumdrop plants, and you'll probably cut off all the unseen flower buds for next year.

■ Prune up large, mounded shrubs to reveal their multistemmed bases. This will add space to the foundation area of the small front garden and show off some nice bark.

■ Take out no more than one-third of a plant's mass each year. Removing more than that could weaken a plant because it makes its food from its leaves. (Renovation is the exception; see "Drastic Renovation" below.)

■ The overall height of a shrub can be reduced by taking the tallest branch out all the way back to where the branch meets a main stem (or to the ground).

Drastic Renovation

Drastic measures can delay the inevitable. Some woody plants can be renovated, which is a polite way of saying "cut down to the ground." Lilacs, rhododendrons, and camellias—all shrubs that may become 10 to 15 feet high and as wide—are good candidates for this treatment. Renovation gives your small front garden a break: the foundation is freed up, and you have more garden space. Leave a trunk about 6 inches high. (This is especially important for lilacs because they used to be—and many still are—grafted onto privet rootstock, and cutting to ground level may trigger the privet to send up shoots of its own.) Drastic renovation will result in the loss of flowers for a few years, in addition to losing sight of the plant. Eventually, of course, you'll again be faced with a large mound of plant. But sometimes it's like starting with a clean slate, and when the new branches start growing, you have a hand in creating the framework of the shrub.

The Porch

The luxury of a porch brings to mind chatting with neighbors and lazy summer evenings. For gardeners with small plots, a porch is also a stage that can be decorated with plants. Containers on porches can soften the look. Stairs lead to porches, which provide you with even more surfaces for pots: on the porch railing (securely anchored, of course) and down each step.

Once again, it's aspect that rules. A porch that faces north may get some direct sun during the summer, but from fall through spring it will be a shady place. East-facing porches have the delight of being in half-day sun; you can grow a lot with that much light. South- and west-facing porches have no relief unless there are trees or screens; otherwise, heavy-duty sun-loving plants are needed there.

Think about how much more garden room steps and a porch give you!

Potted Plants

Wide steps beg for a row of terra-cotta pots up each side, planted with summer annuals. Viny plants such as the black-eyed susan vine *(Thunbergia alata)* are treated as annuals in the Northwest; this one

Far right: **Steps become a floral pathway in the small garden. Snuggled together along the edges here are pots of coleus, fancy-leaved pelargoniums, nasturtiums, and licorice plant (**Helichrysum petiolare **'Limelight').**

has yellow-orange flowers and can be trained up the railings from pots. An easy-care (and less-thirsty) alternative for a sunny porch would be a group of potted hens and chicks *(Sempervivum)* marching up the steps. Pots make it easy to change the scene seasonally, which psychologically makes the small garden seem bigger. It also means you can try marginally hardy plants for summer and fall, and then switch to a winter look. Echeverias are succulent plants similar to hens and chicks, but their flowers can be more colorful—yellow, apricot, orange, and red. Line the steps with 6-inch pots all the way up planted with different echeverias for a colorful look in hot sun. In winter, when hot sun is just a memory, move them to a protected place, such as under the eaves. There, they'll still look good (they are evergreen), and they won't drown in winter rain.

Before you haul a dozen pots around, measure the width of your stairs. A comfortable width for one person to walk up or down is 3 feet. If the steps are too narrow for pots, consider planting below the stairs on either side, and use plants that will billow over the steps. Brushing against fragrant plants such as lemon verbena *(Aloysia triphylla)* or pineapple sage *(Salvia elegans)* as you pass is a pleasant experience—as opposed to dancing around and between pots on steps, trying not to trip.

Some plants are too attractive to bees to be planted near the steps. The blue, fuzzy flowers of the California lilac *(Ceanothus)* are covered in bees in June—the whole plant seems to be buzzing—so save that one for a hot and sunny corner of the garden, where it can take over.

Vines

Use an upright support such as an obelisk or a tepee, and grow a clematis up, over, and around it. Many of these structures are 5 or 6 feet high, and can provide ample vine-viewing as you walk up the steps. Set the obelisk into the ground beside the porch. Metal obelisks have extensions that can be pushed into the soil for stability; wooden tepees may need to be secured with earth staples, which are sold at nurseries.

Early-summer-blooming clematis cultivars typically have wide, flat flowers as big as your head—so big that they can look almost artificial. 'Nelly Moser' is a pale pink with a darker stripe down each petal; 'Pink Champagne' has magenta flowers with a white stripe; and 'The President' blooms in light purple. Those vines all grow to about 10 feet, which is perfect for a small support structure. The more rampant clematis, such as *C. montana* and the evergreen *C. armandii,* need room for their more than 25-foot growth.

The porch framework of railing, sides, and roofline offers ample opportunity for vines. Vines can drip down from the roof and clamber up the downspout. Plant fragrance nearby, so that you can enjoy it coming and going. If you're a porch-sitter, you'll especially appreciate the heady perfume of a climbing honeysuckle wafting your way in summer. Wisteria always seems an obvious choice when you're looking for a fragrant vine, and it does no damage to paint or wood because it twines around rather than attaching itself. But be forewarned: A small garden with an uncontrolled wisteria is, in the end, entirely wisteria.

Hanging Baskets

Hanging baskets provide a visual "top" to your porch, as well as one more place to plant in the small garden. Even an entryway can accommodate one basket, and a porch the length of the house can use more. Hanging baskets are meant to be viewed at eye level as well as from below, so choose plants that will fill the center in addition to those that will dangle from the sides. Most baskets are planted for the season— that is, from spring through fall—and so annuals are often used. Some nurseries have whole tables of "basket fillers" in spring. You can mix and match to your heart's content, filling up on shade plants such as basket fuchsias (always labeled "upright" or "trailing" at the nursery) and hanging begonias. For a basket in the sun, look for some of the new trailing petunias (the Surfina strain), the petunia-like *Calibrachoa* (sold as "Million Bells"), or ivy-leaved geraniums *(Pelargonium).*

Baskets can be of a solid material—wood or plastic—or wire. If you use a wire basket, lined with moss or coir (this coconut-fiber product comes in precut mats), then you can also plant the outside with little mounds of alyssum or some other small clumper.

Hanging baskets, especially the wire kind, dry out in a flash in warm weather. Water twice a day in hot weather, and if the basket dries out too much (and is too difficult to rewet), place it in a shallow pan of water for a while. You can help with watering by placing a perforated piece of PVC piping in the middle of the basket when you plant. (Leave a couple inches of soil under it and surround it with soil and plants.) Fill it with gravel, and water through the pipe; the water will slowly soak into the soil, as opposed to running out the bottom or over the sides. There are specially designed water-holding products on the market that soak up water and, supposedly, release it when the soil is dry. Gardeners have used these with mixed results.

Like other containers, hanging baskets need fertilizer, especially those filled with nonstop bloomers such as fuchsias. At spring planting, incorporate some dry, all-purpose fertilizer (organic or timed-release), and then use a half-strength liquid fertilizer in the water every two weeks (fish fertilizer is good and smells only for a day).

The Entry

In a small garden, the entry is not an afterthought—it may be half of the total front-garden area. Decorating the space around your front door brings the garden just

Below: **A basket of fuchsia hangs at this front door. Fuchsias are workhorses of the small garden, blooming from late spring until frost if kept watered and fertilized.**

about as close as you can to the indoors. It's the last thing you or visitors see before walking through the front door, and it may be the first thing as well, depending on how it's positioned from the street. An entry garden can be planted in the ground, in a built-in raised bed, or in pots.

Balance, Not Symmetry

Aim for balance, not symmetry, in the entry. In the conventional large, formal setting, with the front door exactly in the center of the house, there would be tall, straight yews *(Taxus)*, perfectly matched, flanking the door. Slow-growing, staid yew is about as close as you could come to a perfectly symmetrical look. But usually, the very time we want two plants to look the same is the time that one will be shorter, wider, taller, more yellow, or darker green, or will lose its leaves earlier—even when

they are two cuttings from the same plant. There are too many variables; sun, water, and even soil composition can change every few feet. In other words, in the land of the living there is no perfect match—at least, not for long. And in the close quarters at the front-door entry of a small garden, this would be the first thing that anyone sees.

A better approach would be to create a balance of form and weight. A tall, skinny plant on one side of the door can be balanced on the other side by a ceramic pot planted with a small shrub and mounded perennials. For a doorway that for architectural reasons has only one side available to plant on, you can use a simple planting scheme in the ground or in pots—for example, a small rhododendron for part shade, such as the white-flowered 'Lucy Lou', with *Buxus* 'Green Mountain', which is a conical form of boxwood, at its side. Use something that won't overwhelm one side of the door with weight that can't be matched on the other side. You also won't be taking up too much horizontal space in the small entry.

Built-in Planters

Built-in planters can define the entry space. These planters are usually no more than a foot or two across, a few feet long, and two or three feet high. They can be used for seasonal displays: shade-loving annuals such as *Impatiens* from late spring through summer; cut greens for fall and the holiday season (the advantage being that you can replace branches of pine, cedar, or holly when one batch has started to dry up); and pansies for the rest of the winter. Raised-bed planters bring the garden closer to the eye (a decided advantage if it's shady), so a planting of low-growing annuals doesn't look as flat as it would if it were in the ground.

Left: **Symmetry is difficult to accomplish, and it isn't necessary in an informal garden. Here, plantings at the front door are balanced rather than symmetrical, with a purple-leaved plum on one side and a *Clematis montana* scrambling over the top to weigh down the other side.**

Pots of early bulbs can be sunk into the soil in the planters and changed out when they fade. The palette of plants that live in deep shade is limited, but if you want small evergreens, the best choice would be one of the smaller-growing winter box species, such as *Sarcococca hookeriana* var. *humilis*, which grows to about 2 feet with a low, mounding habit; its 8-foot spread is easily checked by taking out branches.

Framing the Door

Many small front gardens aren't much more than a step or two from the world. Here, it's good to create a small collection of plants that will speak to you and everyone else every day of the year. You don't have to have something in showy bloom in the bleak midwinter; instead, think of the combinations of plants that offer texture, structure, and color long after the sunflowers are finished and before the daffodils bloom. The narrow, upright boxwood *Buxus* 'Graham Blandy' is an evergreen that takes part shade. On the two or three steps leading to the door, cluster pots of auriculas (cultivars of *Primula auricula)*; the plants keep an evergreen rosette of leaves and don't want water in winter, and the various primroselike blooms are showy in early spring—kind of like a Victorian postcard. Sometimes you can have winter pots of things that you intend to plant out in the garden the following spring; for example, you could enjoy one winter's worth of witch-hazel fragrance near the door.

Below: **Shallow spaces can be filled with a variety of plants. Seen here are perennials including dark pink Jupiter's beard (*Centranthus ruber*) and a tall, mauve-pink prairie mallow (*Sidalcea),* while behind the fence is the white hydrangea *Hydrangea arborescens* 'Annabelle'.**

Shade

Shade is often a factor in recessed doorway plantings. In the Pacific Northwest, a north-facing doorway might get a little sunshine during July, but the rest of the year it will be in shade. The entry can feel cavernous, and it certainly won't lend itself to cheery pots of zinnias and sunflowers. Proper plant selection is the answer. Choose small evergreen shrubs that prefer shade, or at least don't mind it, such as heavenly bamboo *(Nandina domestica)*; cultivars are available with a variety of growth habits, including the small, mounded 'Woods Dwarf' and 'Plum Passion', which grows to 5 feet high. *Nandina* also takes dry soil fairly well. If you can water regularly, you can use something like the variegated drooping leucothoë (*Leucothoë fontanesiana* 'Girard's Rainbow'), which has drooping branches that are mottled with cream, pink, and copper. Other *Leucothoë* cultivars are available. Whereas *Nandina* doesn't mind shade, *Leucothoë* demands it.

Pots themselves can brighten dark doorways. What's planted in them doesn't have to be the whole show. A collection of glazed pots with similar patterns, a color theme—all blue and white, for example—or a particular motif can create a single unit, especially if you use similar plants in all the pots. Try mixing sizes of pots, or setting out a row of the same kind. Flamboyant pots of various sizes all can be planted with dwarf evergreens to unify the look.

The Slope

Front gardens with steep slopes are common in the Northwest. Mostly they are planted with grass, which can be quite a challenge when it's time to mow. But there are better things to do with the space if the grass takes a nosedive toward the sidewalk. Whether the slope runs the entire length of a small front garden or just part of it, you can create a garden that won't have to be cut every week.

Selecting and Placing the Plants

Plant the slope with a variety of woody and herbaceous plants. You don't have to change the terrain, but you'll need to pay attention to the selection and placement of the plants. Landscape roses, such as the continuous-blooming pink-flowered 'Bonica', the red 'Fire Meidiland', and 'Grouse', with masses of small, single white flowers, are perfect for slopes, where they can cascade. They are also disease-resistant and hardy. Drawf fragrant sumac (*Rhus aromatica* 'Grow-Low'), a mounding shrub, has glossy green summer foliage and the flaming fall foliage for which sumacs are known. The evergreen ground cover Siberian cypress *(Microbiota decussata)* is a good choice for part shade.

■ Plants at the bottom of the slope will get more water than those at the top, since water runs downhill. Place plants accordingly.

■ Put plants in when they are small, by all means (no sense in digging a hole on a slope for a 5-gallon plant). The hole should be dug so that the rim of the hole is horizontal, not at the angle of the slope.

■ The steeper the slope, the more likely loose mulch will drift down to the bottom and onto the sidewalk. Plants on a slope do need mulch, but don't pile it on too heavily, and sweep the sidewalk occasionally. As the plants grow, their root systems will knit the soil together and their stems will help keep the mulch in place.

Creating a Rockery

Build a rockery up the slope. This provides lots of pockets for plants. Rockeries are heaven for alpine enthusiasts, who collect tiny plants that need the sharp drainage provided by the pockets of soil among large stones.

Alpine plants don't offer much of a multiseason display, however, because they have developed in the wild to take advantage of the extremely short growing season at high elevations.

A rockery needs to be built back into the slope rather than being completely vertical (as does a stacked stone wall). This will help hold the rocks, and it will be easier to form pockets of soil for planting. You can even build little "shelves," using the flattest side of a rock for a horizontal surface. Warmed by the sun, heat-loving plants will flourish.

For a nicely varied rockery garden, choose some plants that have a burst in spring and others that can provide some interesting foliage or flowers for the rest of the year. Perennials suited to rockeries often don't need supplemental water in summer. These include pinks *(Dianthus)*, which in nature grow in rocky, slightly alkaline soil. Species tulips are another good choice; they are small, and they naturalize well, unlike the tall hybrid tulips we are used to. *Lewisia tweedyi*, a Northwest perennial with flowers in shades of peach and pink that is native to mountainous areas, would also appreciate the pockets of warmth and sharp drainage a rockery provides.

Bulbs are fabulous in a rockery, and many of them, such as *Watsonia*, prefer the well-drained soil that rockeries commonly provide. Shorter ornamental onions fit in better than taller species whose stalks—sometimes to 3 feet—can be out of proportion to the rest of the planting. *Allium karativiense* has 5-inch globes of pinkish flowers on stalks only 8 inches high in mid- to late spring. Golden garlic *(A. moly)*, with 2-inch clusters of sunshine-yellow flowers in early summer, grows

Far left: **Plant slopes with a mix of woody and herbaceous plants for interest year-round. Here, the slope includes roses, a purple-leaved Japanese maple, and herbaceous perennials, including spiky purple toad-flax *(Linaria purpurea)* and the tall heads of *Verbena bonariensis*.**

Above: **This strawberry geranium *(Saxifraga stolonifera)* keeps warm and protected against its rock wall.**

10 to 12 inches high. Star of Bethlehem *(Ornithogalum umbellatum)* is another wonderful summer-blooming bulb; it takes part shade, and its white flowers, with a green stripe down the middle of each petal, open in the morning and close in the evening. It is often described as "freely naturalizing," which is a euphemistic term for being invasive. Don't pass over plants such as *Ornithogalum*, though, because what is an aggressive grower to one gardener is the light of another gardener's life. Just know before you plant.

Below: **Terracing a slope makes it easier to plant and maintain. The levels of this stacked stone wall even provide space for a small tree** *(Stewartia pseudocamellia),* **shown here in winter.**

Woody plants that grow as if cascading down a rockery (or a terrace or a retaining wall, for that matter) give the illusion of movement or flow. Low-growing cotoneasters, such as rockspray cotoneaster *(Cotoneaster microphyllus),* offer a fine texture with their small leaves; cotoneasters also have showy red berries in winter to brighten the scene. Another small berried shrub, *Sorbus reducta,* has small clusters of pink-red berries that hold on into early winter. This ground cover grows up to 2 feet in height and spreads underground. If you are reluctant to choose spreading plants for the level areas of your small garden, a rockery would be an ideal place for one or two, since a plant in a planting pocket often has nowhere else to go.

Terracing the Slope

Terracing can change a slope into several flat levels. This means cutting into the slope to create level surfaces that look like stairsteps. The front edge of each level can be held up with a row of bricks or a few layers of stacked stone—it doesn't have to be an engineering marvel. Terraces make watering much easier because the water won't run down the hillside. Make each planting level at least 2 feet deep from front to back, or you won't have much room to grow. And plant closely enough that the bark or compost mulch doesn't visually dominate the slope.

Even small terraced slopes need stepping-stones so that you can walk down to each level. The stepping-stones aren't there for show, but to make maintenance easier and to protect the plants. With seasonal displays, it's hard to remember what is planted where; summer bulbs are late to come up, some winter-blooming plants disappear by July, and if you don't have every inch of your garden memorized, it's wonderful to know that you can put your foot there, and not damage anything.

Using Retaining Walls

A retaining wall is a blank slate. It fairly begs for plants to tumble over the edge and cascade down, or for vines to climb up the façade. Prominent features of hilly neighborhoods with small gardens, retaining walls can be 2 to 5 feet high; the higher the wall, the blanker the slate. Retaining walls can be solid poured concrete or can look like stone walls. They differ from dry stacked-stone walls in that they are actually all of one piece, well mortared.

If the wall faces west or south, it will be a heat factory, baking anything that dares grow there. Take advantage of the heat (from the sun and radiating from the wall) by choosing plants that like a little baking. Hanging off the edge, try a prostrate rosemary (*Rosmarinus officinalis* 'Huntington Carpet' or 'Prostratus'), or clumps of clove-scented pinks, such as *Dianthus* 'Inchmery', which love limey concrete. At the base of the wall, espalier a tree anemone *(Carpenteria californica),* known for its large, white, fragrant flowers that appear in summer. Or, if there's scant space between the base of the wall and the sidewalk, choose a row of tall skinny plants, such as small conifers.

If the wall faces east or north, it can be a chilly, dark, dank spot. North-facing walls can be a challenge, but there are plants that prefer cooler circumstances. Self-clinging silver-vein creeper *(Parthenocissus henryana)*, like other members of its genus, climbs by means of suckers that stick to surfaces (rather than aerial roots, which would invade and crumble masonry). The foliage of *P. henryana*, a deciduous vine, opens red in spring and turns scarlet in fall; between times, the five-fingered leaves show a silvery stripe down each leaflet. Other plants that work well include cultivars of heavenly bamboo (*Nandina domestica*—a plant that works in so many situations, it is all things to all gardeners) and yew *(Taxus)*.

Build Your Own Wall

The art of building stone walls is an ancient one, stemming from the need to clear rocky fields for crops and to keep live-stock in and wild beasts out. Low stone walls are still a feature in Ireland, where the ground seems to grow rocks better than anywhere else. If you have a short slope, 2 feet high or less, you may want to build your own retaining wall out of stacked stone. Higher walls, and those where you'll need to deal with water, natural gas, and sewer lines, are best left to engineers. A short wall, 2 feet high or so, is a project within the reach of most gardeners, and can be made easier by using flat stones (purchased) instead of rocks that need to be fitted together like a jigsaw puzzle. Even a 2-foot wall, if it's made from loose stone, needs to be angled back into the bank to prevent the top layer of stones from eventually being pushed out by the soil. It's a good idea to mortar the top layer of the stones for safety. With a stacked stone wall, you don't have to worry about how even the top is—just tuck plants behind the top stones and they'll grow out and over, disguising any bumps.

The Corner Lot

The corner lot doubles your exposure to the world—it's like having two front gardens, even if you have only one front door. If both exposed sides are planted the same, it may indeed look as though there are two front doors. Clearly defining the front helps visitors know where to go. It also gives the garden the illusion of more space, with room perhaps for roses in front and daylilies along the side.

With a small front garden, you often think of ways either to hide from or to invite in the public. If your house is in the middle of the block, the windows need to be screened by plants only on one side. With two sides to deal with, you not only have twice the public exposure to think about, you may also have foot traffic cutting across your property.

Anchoring the Corner

A tree at the corner will visually anchor your property, and it can also serve as a landmark when you're giving directions to visitors. More than that, it's particularly valuable on a corner where your landscape is flat and it's easy for walkers to cut corners. Plant something low-branching but not wide, such as the columnar purple beech *Fagus sylvatica* 'Dawyck Purple' or the narrow Western red cedar *Thuja plicata* 'Hogan'. A deciduous tree with a wider canopy can allow for under-planting that will block foot traffic, while still not taking up space in the garden. Japanese maples are a good choice because their finely textured foliage adds lightness to the garden, instead of adding bulk.

An elevated corner can still benefit from a shrub or a small tree. To keep garden and house in scale, don't plant a tall tree on a high corner if your house is small. Instead, choose a medium-sized shrub or small tree. If the corner receives shade from nearby buildings or larger neighboring trees, use the graceful mountain hemlock, *Tsuga mertensiana*. One of the most beautiful Northwest natives, it has a loose, conical habit that suits our gardens and our climates.

A raised corner, either as a part of a rockery that wraps around the property or as a pinnacle formed by two rising sides, is a perfect place to plant a cascading rose, such as the almost-nonstop-blooming 'Bonica'.

Or use a vine as half ground cover, half climber—either a clematis or, excellent in shade, the silver-veined *Parthenocissus henryana*.

Using Fences or Barrier Hedges

A hedge or fence along one side clearly defines the space yet leaves the front garden open. A screen on one side of your corner blocks the view of the bus stop, neighboring business, or busy street. Remember that you're just trying to keep people out, not attack them; thorny shrubs such as firethorn *(Pyracantha)* and barberry *(Berberis)*, for example, would not be good choices unless they were trained against the fence. Sidewalks must not be blocked, and if you plant a hedge that grows too wide for its space, you'll have to keep up with trimming or it might be trimmed for you—by the city or even by citizen pruners who have gotten tired of being whacked in the face by branches.

Below: **Although it's only a temporary hedge, this thick planting of the 5-foot annual white shooting stars** *(Nicotiana sylvestris)* **keeps summer foot traffic at bay and provides evening fragrance.**

A fence is a reasonable way to deal with traffic. Check with your city on how close to the sidewalk a fence is allowed. Property lines usually begin a foot or so behind the sidewalk, so if you end up with a bare 6 to 12 inches between fence and sidewalk, this strip will become a haven for weeds and trash. Consider planting a thick row of tiny evergreen shrubs to fill in that space. Small boxwood cultivars, such as *Buxus* 'Tiny Tim', boxlike *Paxistima canbyi*, or the thorny rosemary barberry *Berberis stenophylla* 'Nana Compacta', would all suit; the first two are especially valuable in part-shade situations. (More on fences and hedges in Chapter Four.)

Don't build a fortress without a way to get in. If you or your guests park on the street, you'll need to provide a gate or some other opening. Unless you want to shut the world out completely, consider a gate with a cutout at eye level or one that has openwork at the top. (For more on gates, see Chapter Three.)

The Planting Strip

Below: **Planting strips mean valuable extra space in the small garden. Taking advantage of its full-sun exposure, this planting strip is filled with sun-loving Mexican feather grass** *(Stipa tenuissima),* **Russian sage** *(Perovskia atriplicifolia),* **Sedum 'Autumn Joy',** **and lavender.**

The narrow strip of garden between sidewalk and street is, in many ways, no-man's-land. It's the farthest from the house, the least accessible with the hose, and impractical for an installed sprinkler system. The small front garden between the sidewalk and the house may look fabulous, but if a sad, neglected bit of weedy grass is its introduction, then the impact is lessened. More and more, gardeners with small properties are taking this bit of land and making it part of the garden, either with trees or with low-water-use plants.

Designing Your Planting Strip

What would you like this new small garden to be? It's difficult to keep people from walking across or parking in front of this strip, so put aside any visions you have of planting an impenetrable thorny mass or building a 2-foot-high raised bed. The planting strip needs to be an accommodating garden, making way for neighbors and traffic while providing you with more places to put plants. It's far enough away from the rest of the garden that style or design doesn't have to be carried over. You're free to do what you want.

Some cities have guidelines for planting strips. Even if your city doesn't, these suggestions make sense:

■ Don't plant anything that grows more than 3 feet high (2 feet on a corner lot). This is a safety issue—not only do you need to see cars coming, drivers need to see children before they dart out into the street.

■ Don't build raised beds. Think about opening your car door into one of those.

■ Provide at least one path from street to sidewalk (unless you don't mind passersby creating one for you).

Choosing Appropriate Plants

Soil in the planting strip is not the best, to put it mildly. The planting strip usually consists of the dregs of the soil; compacted from foot traffic and road construction, it is silty and drains poorly. Dig in compost and mound up slightly wherever you can. The act of planting a variety of species from annuals to shrubs will help to enrich the soil over time, because even living plants slough off cells from roots and drop leaves that break down into humus for the soil.

Be realistic about water. As tempting as it might be to plant some showy iris, a small rose garden, shrubby willows, or a delicate astilbe out there, all of these plants need regular water, so they're inappropriate to an area where the hose doesn't reach. Good mulching will not only keep down weeds but conserve moisture in the soil, which helps with your no-water rule.

Look for plants that need full sun. This is the most likely situation you'll have in the planting strip, so it's best to stick with tough plants that, once established, don't require extensive summer watering. The Mediterranean look—sans sand—is one that is well suited to these small areas, and that includes many plants with silver foliage, which are usually native to dry, hot, sunny climates.

■ *Artemisia* is a fine example. Shrubby selections include lacy-leaved *A.* 'Powis Castle' and 'Lambrook Silver' (the former grows 3 feet high and as wide, the latter a little larger). *A.* 'Silver Queen' and 'Valerie Finnis' are suckering perennials with lance-shaped silver leaves. *A. schmidtiana* 'Silver Mound' is an herbaceous perennial that grows into a silver and silky-soft mound of foliage (which is best cut back hard in early spring so that it doesn't "open up" in the middle).

■ Lavenders, especially smaller ones such as 'Hidcote' and 'Martha Roderick', stay below 2 feet. Culinary sage *(Salvia officinalis)* also does well under these conditions, and several cultivars are available. 'Berggarten' has large leaves; the foliage of 'Aurea Variegata' is variegated with gold; 'Tricolor' has cream and pink tones to its leaves.

■ Choose evergreen plants (or those with winter interest in stems and seed heads) as often as possible. The planting-strip garden is on display year-round.

■ Ground-cover thymes (woolly, creeping, and others) spread well over hot sunny areas and around stepping-stones.

■ Some dwarf conifers (especially cultivars of Hinoki cypress *Chamaecyparis obtusa*) prefer full sun, and their presence throughout winter adds the all-important "bones"—a term that refers to a year-round structural presence—to the garden.

■ Rock roses (*Cistus* spp.) also prefer it hot and dry; low-growing *C.* x *skanbergii* has gray-green leaves and small pink flowers in early summer.

Trees in the Small Garden

It's always the tree's fault, never our own. It's too big. It's too wide. How did it get that tall? A branch is scraping the house, or creating too much shade, or coming too close to the wires. How dare the tree grow that big?

It is our responsibility as gardeners to choose wisely; this can't be said often enough (apparently), and it's particularly true in the small garden, where almost everything is on display almost all the time. If we know a tree will outgrow its site, then we should choose another kind of tree, or be prepared to give the tree away to a good home before it reaches critical mass. But even so, there are times when a tree needs to be pruned for one reason or another—although none of those reasons should be to "shape" the tree. The tree knows what shape it's supposed to be.

Below: **The Japanese snowbell tree** *(Styrax japonicum)* **is a good choice for the small garden whether it's planted along the street or by the house. Delicate, white bell flowers in June give way to green, marble-sized fruits later in the summer.**

Pruning

Pruning trees is a scary affair for a gardener, or at least it should be. No one should take a pruning saw and start whacking away, willy-nilly, without some cautious and serious forethought. More damage has been done—and not just to the tree—by improper pruning than by not pruning at all. So, consider these pruning basics before you make the cut:

■ If the job seems too big or too serious, call a certified arborist. A certified arborist is a professional who is trained to know how to evaluate and deal with hazardous or diseased trees. A certified arborist is almost never the "tree guy" who drives down your street looking for easy prey (and I don't mean the tree).

■ Certified arborists can prune conifers to help lighten your small garden, giving it an open woodland feel. They limb up and thin out some of the branches. This also helps the trees deal with strong winds; with the density decreased, the wind can pass through branches instead of hitting the canopy as though it were a solid wall.

■ Competent certified arborists will never suggest that you top a tree, nor will they do it if you ask. Some gardeners incorrectly think that tree topping—slicing off the top part of a tree—helps keep the tree from falling over on your house. (The euphemistic term "view pruning" is also topping.) Topping weakens the tree and leads to the trunk rotting, which can cause a problem much more serious than the fact that you can't see the lake.

■ If the job is within your physical means, learn the three basic D's of pruning: take out dead, diseased, or dying limbs first. (See the pruning guidelines earlier in this chapter, on page 40.)

Street-Tree Lists

A list of recommended street trees is one of the most useful tools you can find. Street-tree lists from cities and towns in the Northwest contain species that grow well in our climate, and, in addition, are able to take some abuse. Cities and towns have had to, by necessity, pare down all the trees that are hardy in their regions to those that meet certain qualifications, and many of those same qualifications are just as useful to keep in mind when you're choosing a tree for the interior of a small garden. Decades ago, broad, spreading trees were planted along boulevards, especially in hot-weather areas. Their canopies provided shade for the street as well as the front yards of the houses or the fronts of businesses. In today's neighborhoods, and in our small gardens, there is seldom room for large trees, and several considerations need to be kept in mind.

City street-tree lists categorize trees by height—small trees to 30 feet, medium trees to 40 feet, and—chosen less and less in our tightening cities—large trees to 50 feet and above. For your parking strip, be sure to choose a tree that will stay short enough to grow under utility lines. Trees on these lists are also usually narrow in form (or if not, the list will tell you how wide they do grow). The lists shy away from trees that have problems with aphids (which drop sticky honeydew on cars and sidewalks below), have surface roots, or are prone to broken branches. (Bigleaf maple, *Acer macrophyllum*, is a majestic tree, but huge branches can come crashing to the ground in windstorms.)

The trees chosen for these lists are tough—a primary consideration because city trees are under constant stress. These trees can grow in a limited amount of soil. Just think—the roots of a tree planted next to the street grow under the street and sidewalk. The soil is often compacted, seldom receives fertilizer, gets watered by a truck in the summer, and has car exhaust wafting up around its foliage day and night. To have to put up with all that, you'd think the trees on the list would resemble concrete poles—tough as nails, but hardly decorative. Instead, here are some of your possible choices:

■ Lovely spring-flowering trees such as Korean dogwood (*Cornus kousa* 'Milky Way'), which has large white flowers (actually leafy structures called bracts) and knobby red fruit, and Cleveland pear (*Pyrus calleryana* 'Cleveland Select'), which grows upright, has strong branches, and is resistant to fire blight.

■ Trees with handsome summer foliage, such as hornbeams (*Carpinus betula* 'Fastigiata') and beech trees (*Fagus sylvatica* 'Dawyck').

■ Trees that display glorious fall color, such as scarlet maple (*Acer rubrum* 'Red Sunset' is a common choice) and paperbark maple *(Acer griseum),* which also provides winter interest with its peeling, cinnamon-colored bark. All this and under 30 feet—such a bargain!

For the recommended street-tree list in your city, call the parks department, the urban forester if there is one, or the transportation or utilities department (because they are the ones who have to deal with trees under power lines, they often have a say in what gets planted).

The Noisy Garden

Living closer together means that we are closer to streets, traffic, and the accompanying noise. It would be wonderful if there were a particular plant (named, perhaps, *Decibelia loweratus*) that would absorb all noise coming from without, leaving the front garden a peaceful and tranquil place.

Unfortunately, there is no magic plant—although you wouldn't know it from the talk. Hedges are commonly recommended to reduce noise, but there is little to no scientific evidence that actual decibel level is lowered. What happens instead is that we perceive the noise to be lower because we can't see what is making it. So it doesn't hurt to put in a tight row of evergreens (although it doesn't help much either). A solid fence may help slightly, but sound has a way of wafting over the top of a fence and hitting you smack in the face.

If you spend time in your front garden and want to enjoy the experience instead of listening for the next Number 7 bus to stop right outside your gate, then distraction is the best way around noise. Plant a hedge that will mask the traffic noise with noise of its own. The sound of bamboo, rustling in the breeze, is a good defense against unwanted sound. Bamboo scares some gardeners; there are always horror stories of bamboo taking over a garden, and any recommendation to plant it usually comes with a list of ways to keep it under control. Choose clumping bamboo (cultivars of *Bambusa multiplex* and *Fargesia* spp., for example), instead of running bamboo, and ask at the nursery about all the things you can do to keep it in its place (there are those warnings again). For every gardener worried about bamboo, there are two who wouldn't be without it.

Below: **The sound of water from the fountain in this small front garden helps mask the traffic noise just beyond the fence.**

Water is another way to divert your attention from unwanted noise, but a still pond won't do the trick—there must be movement from a fountain. A visit to a garden center or a specialty water-garden nursery will help you decide what kind of water sound you like best. Some fountains burble, others drip, and still others sound as though you're pouring lemonade into a huge glass. Maybe you could take along a tape of an engine revving up to help you decide which fountain works for you.

The Downspout Garden

Space is tight in the small garden, so it's hard to give up any bit of ground that could possibly be planted. The area immediately around the downspouts would seem like a perfect place for a tall, narrow shrub; but the soil can easily be washed away from roots by water gushing out the downspout, and when it's dry, this beaten-up soil is hard and compacted. Decrease the rainwater's power and help with drainage by using rocks around the downspout. Large rocks will create a splash, but a small area of various-sized stones collected from the garden will do the job. These will decrease soil erosion, protect plant roots, and help with drainage, especially if you create a small streambed leading away from the house (the water will follow the easier path of moving through the rocks).

Choose plants that won't mind a rock mulch, and you will be able to use this garden space. If the exposure is right, plant clematis, known for wanting their feet in the shade and their heads in the sun; the rocks will help keep the soil cool. If the downspout is in full sun, consider a planting of the dwarf redtwig dogwood, *Cornus stolonifera* 'Kelseyi', which grows to only 18 inches and suckers slightly in moist soil. Its bare but colorful stems will brighten up the winter. In part shade, plant a bold *Rodgersia*, such as the bronze-leaf *R. pinnata*, which grows to 3 feet. Ferny astilbes like extra moisture, as does the cardinal flower *(Lobelia cardinalis)*.

Chapter Three

- **Gates**
- **Arbors**
- **Foundation Plantings**
- **Paths**
- **Planting the Narrow Side Garden**
- **The Other Side Garden**

Left: **The openwork of this iron gate acts as a boundary yet also invites you to look past the oakleaf hydrangea (*Hydrangea quercifolia*) to the garden beyond.**

The Side Garden and Pathways

The small side garden is often no more than a pathway from front to back. With little room, and the neighbors looming over you, it's easy to think that the best thing to do would be to build a tall fence or plant a dense-growing, evergreen screen—anything for a little privacy. But if part of your house looks out onto the side garden—perhaps the kitchen window, or a nook in the dining room—you'll want to have a pleasant vignette in your view, not just a solid wall of green. A good garden, no matter how narrow, contains a variety of plants, suited to the conditions, with something to offer at all times of the year.

Too often the small side garden is an afterthought—a worn path that slips around the corner and runs along the house until it empties you out into the back. A pain to mow, because it's such a narrow strip; too narrow, it would seem, to be a garden. It's the part of your property that is squeezed into a corridor; much used, but often not really noticed. With a beginning, middle, and end defined by structures such as arbors and gates, it becomes more than just a trampled path between house and hedge; it becomes a garden.

Functions of Side Gardens

Side gardens can be valuable transition zones. The side garden can help you change styles—say, from romantic Victorian in front to tropical oasis in back. Or you may be forced to change styles and plantings because the conditions demand it; perhaps the front is sunny and the back is shady, or the front is exposed to the world but the back is a private retreat. The side garden can moderate such changes.

Give yourself room to move. In the narrow space between your house and the fence, you need to be able to walk comfortably, transport the garbage and recycling, haul bags of compost and pots of plants. You need a fairly even surface, and enough elbow room so that getting through isn't a battle. The space is most likely already defined (by the house and the fence), and there is little you can do about it without picking up your house and moving it a few feet. The side garden is an area where form and function collide more crucially than in larger spaces. Everything needs to work. The plants, path, gates, and arbors that you use here can help disguise and decorate this utilitarian space.

Planting space is at a premium everywhere in the small garden, but the small side garden seems to have little to none. Against the house and under the eaves, it's dry and shady (or burning up in the sun); plants perish before they can establish. Every plant you like grows too wide for the area, billowing out onto the path either at your feet (tripping you up) or higher (smacking you in the face) as you walk through. In the Pacific Northwest, narrow spaces between buildings offer more shade than sun in all but the long days of high summer, but it isn't unheard of to have too much sun in the strip alongside the house.

The side garden may even constitute a sizable chunk of your total garden space; depending on where the house is situated on the property, the side garden, as small as it is, could be the main show. Take advantage of any gardening area that you have. You'll be able to do more than you think.

Gates

The path around the side of your house has a beginning and an end (and in the small garden, these aren't far from each other), and to emphasize the space you can use one or two gates or arbors. A gate at the beginning and another at the end of the side garden make a statement that this is indeed a separate place, helping to make the small garden seem larger. Even a gate at only one end will help—it can keep people and dogs in or out, or at least slow them down and make it easier for you to keep your eye on them. Such gates, fully functional, are an extension of the fence, and create the third and fourth walls of the side garden.

Use gates at both ends only if there is enough room. The walk needs to be long enough to let you open and close the gates at each end without feeling as though you are turning around in circles. Any area shorter than 10 feet that has a front and back gate will seem as if it's all gate and no garden.

Freestanding Gates

Sometimes a gate is just for show, to act only as a visual divider between two spaces. If that is the case, no fence is necessary—or at least connecting the gate to the fence isn't necessary. What is necessary is to make the freestanding gate an integral part of the scene. A freestanding gate, secured with its own postholes, can stand out like a sore thumb unless it is woven into the fabric of the garden with plants, and at least visually connected to the fence and house in style. A rustic gate made from woven branches would look incongruous next to an ultramodern house but would be right at home with an older-looking house in the Arts and Crafts style. Owners of huge estates can indulge a whim by placing such mismatched elements far enough apart so that it doesn't matter, but in the small garden, a Japanese pagoda–style gate sits uncomfortably next to an English Tudor house. The outline of the gate doesn't necessarily have to echo the outline of your roof, but matching rustic with rustic, Asian with Asian, and formal with formal will bring coherence to the small garden rather than chopping it up into bits.

Gate Styles

Gates vary widely in type, and the gate in the small side garden can make an artistic statement as well as a statement of purpose. A see-through scrim of pickets or of thin one-by-one pieces of lumber is the least confining, allowing an almost unrestricted view of what's behind it. For the natural, weathered look, gates (and fences) in the Northwest are often made from Western red cedar; its new-wood look ages to a comfortable silvery gray.

More formal or classic styles are made of iron, and you can find foundries that will build a gate from your own design. For something that establishes more of a boundary yet is still inviting, a 4-foot-high

Below: **This small side garden is a shady oasis from front to back. Although it's narrow, there is room for ground covers, shrubs, and, at the sunny end, a gate with a rose-covered arbor.**

gate gives that over-the-back-fence feel, a halfway invitation to stop and check out what's inside. The most private kind of gate, tall and made of solid wood or metal, will stop any inquisitive eyes from taking a peek—most useful if your small garden is easily seen from a busy sidewalk. But even that style can be softened just a bit if it has an eye-level cutout—a whimsical touch that shows you don't mind a little company.

The small garden gives you the opportunity to show off art on an intimate scale, and the flat surface of a wooden gate can be the perfect blank canvas. You can grow something alongside or on the post of a gate, but a plant that tried to grow up the actual surface of the gate would speedily be discouraged by the gate's opening and closing, so this is where artwork comes in. Commission an artist friend to paint a morning glory on the gate and you'll never be without flowers in the garden. Or choose a piece of art, such as a ceramic sun face in relief, and mount it on the gate.

Arbors

An arbor at each end of a side garden is another way of signaling the beginning and end without all the bother of latches and swinging gates. An arbor has a more welcoming feel to it—after all, you can walk right through. Arbors provide another home for plants, whether they be climbing roses or honeysuckle. They also stop the eye from its visual trek straight through the small garden by drawing the gaze upward. Anything that lets the eye linger in one place makes the small garden seem larger. But visual "tricks" in the small garden need to be uncomplicated to work best.

Arbors as Frames

Arbors frame the view beyond. A fountain, a sculpture, or a special small tree that is placed on an axis with the arbor is framed, drawing the viewer's attention to it. It becomes instant "artwork."

A pair of arbors (or an arbor with a gate beyond, as you would have at the beginning and end of the side garden) create depth, and thus make the garden look larger. The visual division makes us think that the space beyond is big enough to separate, and the separate structures lead the eye on. It's the simplest of visual tricks and works no matter which end you're standing at. However, the arbors shouldn't be two different sizes. That Alice-in-Wonderland trick won't work, because the perspective isn't the same from both directions. Making the far arbor smaller may make it look farther away, but when you are standing under the small arbor, the larger arbor will appear closer—defeating your purpose.

If you use a fence with an opening, try leaving the gate open (or not having one at all, just a wide gap), and use fencing material that is somewhat open, such as pickets. If you then have a focal point beyond that—a sundial or an obelisk—the eye is drawn through one section (the side garden), through another entry (a gate or another arbor), and beyond to the object. Your garden will "grow."

Arbor Styles

Arbors, like gates, come in many styles. Just like a gate, an arbor fits the small garden best when it's in harmony with the style around it— the house, the fence, the garden. A rounded archway has a softer, romantic feel to it than does a flat-topped arbor, especially the kind with a pagoda look, in which the top pieces of wood extend beyond the supports on both sides; those have an Asian feel to the design. A wooden arbor can even have a small roof, although this precludes any vines reaching the top. Metal arbors usually have a more airy, less heavy look, because the pieces are thinner and don't block as much of the view, and some are artistically adorned with vines and leaves of their own. An arbor made from a single arched bar or piece of wood is simple and minimal; At the other end of the scale are structures at least 2 feet deep with latticework or other fancy work between the front and the back—these are the double-wides of arbors.

Vines and Climbing Roses

Take advantage of arbors as one of many vertical spaces in the small garden. But if you expect people to walk under an arbor, then choose your vines appropriately. An arbor, when installed, will be about 8 feet high at its apex, and perhaps a foot or so deep. Vines and climbing roses that grow to 10 or even 15 feet would be good choices; you could plant one on each side of the arbor. Some vines are too rampant for an arbor; for example, the chocolate vine *(Akebia quinata)* grows to 30 feet and does so quickly. An *Akebia* on an arbor would either attempt to grab passersby or have to be on a strict pruning schedule—and what's the point of purposely adding a high-maintenance plant to that part of your landscape? Give the *Akebia* an entire fence or garage, and look to other vines for your arbor.

The combination of roses and clematis on an arbor is irresistible, and the plants provide a lot of show for a small space. It's even more impressive if you choose a repeat-blooming rose, such as the delicately pink 'New Dawn', or the warm apricot tones of 'Westerland'. In the

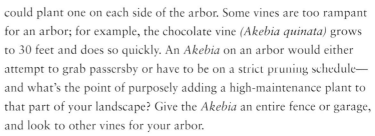

Northwest, some continuously flowering roses, such as the English roses, will bloom into December in mild years. Clematis can also extend the flowering season. Some varieties that bloom in early summer may repeat sporadically later, but even more impressive are cultivars of *Clematis viticella*, such as 'Etoile Violette', with deep purple flowers, that have their bloom-time beginning in August and extending into fall. The flowers themselves may not be as large as those of a June-blooming type that blooms again lightly in late fall, but they are reliable and easy, and they come at a time when much of the flowering part of the garden is slowing down.

The word "climber" can be deceptive, especially when it comes to roses. In small spaces, we must be diligent about selecting the plants we grow, because some could end up being as big as the entire garden. Climbing roses in nature grow up into trees—such sturdy woody supports—and don't hold onto much of anything. Their

Below: **The back garden is seen here framed by a flat-topped arbor. The contrast between the shady side garden and the sunny back garden makes the picture beyond stand out even more.**

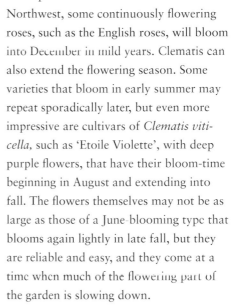

thorns help them catch onto bark, and the long canes are eventually held up by whatever they grow into. Often rambling and climbing roses are grouped into the "climber" category, but they do have some differences. Usually "ramblers" have smaller flowers, borne profusely in clusters, and are more vigorous growers. 'Cecile Brunner' is a charming, old-fashioned rambler that is covered in clusters of soft pink flowers in June; it can grow to 20 feet. "Climbers" (which are sometimes sports of nonclimbing roses) are often larger-flowered and don't grow as big.

Some roses that are not classified as climbers at all may, if left to their own devices, reach 8 feet, and so would do well running up the

Below: **Clematis make perfect arbor plants. Here, the yellow bells of golden clematis (***Clematis tangutica***'Lemon Bells')
scramble over an archway.**

side of an arbor. 'Galway Bay' is a pink-flowered climber that repeats; it grows to about 10 feet. 'Graham Thomas', one of the roses from the English breeder David Austin, has clusters of large, deep yellow flowers and will bloom until winter. Although classified as a shrub rose, it will grow to 10 feet and so can be used as a climber.

A new and lesser-known category of climbing roses, and one that is perfect for the small garden, is the patio climber (sometimes called miniature climber). These roses grow up to 10 feet tall and bloom in clusters of small flowers. These small-scale roses offer gardeners the chance to have a climbing rose growing out of a pot on the deck or running up one side of an arbor. Two examples are 'Warm Welcome', which has fragrant orange flowers, and 'Laura Ford', with yellow flowers flushed with amber.

Support Your Vine

Plants grow upward to get to light, and vining plants, whose natural habitats are often forests, have developed ways to hold onto other plants for support in their climb to the sun. They do it in a variety of ways, though, and in the small garden you don't need vines flopping about on top of other plants (unless you've planned it that way). You need to know what style of climber you have so that you are prepared with proper supports in place if necessary.

■ Clematis vines twine their leaf stems (called petioles) around a support, so give them supports thin enough for a good hold. Because the petioles can range from 2 to 4 inches long, a clematis can't climb a fence made of 6-inch-wide boards, but it will happily scramble up a trellis made of 1-inch lumber.

■ Sweet peas, an annual, climb by sending out thin tendrils, which are actually modified leaves, to twine around something.

■ Members of the grape family also climb by way of tendrils. The decorative variegated porcelain vine (*Ampelopsis brevipedunculata* 'Elegans') has cream-splashed leaves and clusters of blue berries, which are beautiful but inedible.

■ Beans twine their entire stem around a stake.

■ Creepers, such as *Parthenocissus* spp., grow small pads that adhere to solid surfaces.

Help out new vines by placing the supports as low to the ground as needed—an 18-inch-gap between ground and twine is a long stretch for a sweet pea. Tie up vines that don't twist or twine. Use a soft material for ties. Wire can cut into stems; buy green garden tape, or use dark sisal twine or (and it's been done many times) strips of old pantyhose.

Foundation Plantings

Below: The silver-leaved *Lamium* 'Hermann's Pride' grows in well-behaved clumps, but the variegated bishop's weed (*Aegopodium podagraria* 'Variegata') is a rampant grower under ideal conditions. That makes it a perfect candidate for a narrow strip of soil where it has nowhere else to go except where you want it.

One side of the path through the side garden is the strip of soil that runs up against the foundation of the house. This is often terrible soil. Hard, rocky, and difficult to dig, it seems to be part concrete (and may actually be so). And, because it's under the eaves of the house, it's dry most of the time. But open ground is valuable in the small side garden, and because there's no way to avoid walking through it, it's necessary to find some rugged plants that look good in the space and meet all the requirements. You want something that won't 1) flop onto the walk, 2) run under the foundation, 3) need watering (something you're not supposed to do up next to the foundation), or 4) make a general nuisance of itself.

Use Tough Plants

Look for plants with tough constitutions. This may mean choosing a plant that, in other parts of the garden, might be called a thug; in the poor conditions of the typical side garden, such plants stay in check yet remain chipper. London pride (listed as *Saxifraga umbrosa* or *S.* x *urbium*) may seem to be almost too common in Northwest gardens, but that's because it does well with minimum care. Its succulent leaves grow in rosettes, and new rosettes are held tightly against the mother plant, creating a solid ground cover. It even comes in a variegated form (*S. umbrosa* 'Variegata'). A moist, well-drained, sunny location suits it, but in that narrow band of no-plant's-land it still grows well, providing good ground cover and handsome evergreen foliage. Its spring flowers, on thin stalks rising 18 inches above the foliage, are fine but almost superfluous. Other choices include a selection of carpet bugle (such as *Ajuga pyramidalis* 'Metallica Crispa') and lily turf (*Liriope muscari*).

Use Edging Plants

Edging plants are good for this slip of a garden. *Alchemilla alpina*, a small lady's mantle with silver-edged leaves (the silver comes from tiny hairs), is a low, mounding plant that doesn't mind neglect. In shade, the leaf stems are more elongated, but the looser mound is charming too. It will reseed between cracks if you leave the small sprays of greenish flowers, but it won't try to take over. Beach strawberry *(Fragaria chiloensis),* a Northwest native, would prefer cushier circumstances but will grow in a difficult side garden, and it makes a clean statement with its glossy, dark green leaves and red stems. It hops around, rooting and forming small plants just as other strawberries do. If you get flowers (and that's not a sure thing), they will be white, followed by seedy strawberries that the birds will love (beach strawberry is one of the parents of our cultivated strawberries).

Avoid These Plants

- Ferns and any other plants that need constant moisture.

- Tall herbaceous perennials that will collapse over the path and turn into trip wires.

- Anything woody that grows more than 10 inches wide.

Paths

Having a reliable, fairly dry, and fairly level place to walk in the garden—even during wet Northwest winters—takes our mind off safety and lets us pay attention to plants and enjoy the garden experience. The path is a guide, keeping us out of the mud and off tender plants that wouldn't appreciate our heavy feet. In large gardens, paths can meander for no apparent reason except to showcase plants. In the small garden, paths are both utilitarian and decorative.

Once again, avoid visual trickery, which will only backfire in the end. Some books recommend that you build the path so that it narrows slightly at the far end. This gives the illusion that the path is longer than it is, but only when you are looking at it from the wide end. Perspective may work in a theater, where the audience sees the stage from only one side, but when your garden visitors are standing at the far end, the path (and your side garden) will look shorter, not longer.

Whether you're redoing an existing path or creating a new one, there are practical choices in materials and plants that will give the small side garden its own identity.

Tips for Path-Making:

■ Two feet wide is the minimum for one person to walk comfortably down a path; three feet wide is better but not always possible where space is at a premium.

■ Inevitably, footsteps wander off the beaten path, especially when you've limited the walking space. Whether the path is solid material or stepping-stones, either keep plants out of the way or choose plants that can withstand foot traffic.

■ If there is room, let the style of the garden dictate the width of the path. The more informal, the narrower the path can be (within reason), with plants billowing out. It may feel charming to casually brush back a branch, but fighting to get through is tedious.

Choosing the Path Material

Choose a path material that is functional in a small space and suits your style, whether casual or formal. Although there is seldom room for a winding path in the narrow side garden, a straight line doesn't have to be strictly formal. A poured concrete sidewalk is a solid, no-nonsense affair, but using chunks of recycled concrete instead breaks down the formality. Grass paths—those wide swaths of green so beautifully separating huge herbaceous borders in photos of English gardens—are impractical in a side garden that gets a lot of foot traffic. The soil in a narrow 2-foot path will become compacted; the grass will wear thin and, in normally dry Northwest summers, will brown out without constant watering. If you prefer grass, place stepping-stones to take the brunt of heavy feet; then the effect will be green and grassy without the wear and tear. Turf, remember, needs to be cut.

Paths can be soft and quiet or pleasantly crunchy underfoot. Every material has its good and bad points, so it's up to you to decide what kind of a look you want, and how you want to maintain it. Solid walkways, a more formal look, are more work to put in but last a long time; casual, loose material is easy to install but seems to disappear over time as it gets walked or scuffed away.

There's such a variety of materials for paths that you may want to spend some time looking underfoot when you're in other people's gardens, public gardens, and nurseries to see what you like. Take into account the length and width of your path in the small side garden. Paths that are only a few steps long will look better and be easier to create with stepping-stones rather than excavating to lay loose material or mortaring bricks.

Below: **These concrete aggregate stepping-stones are a good choice for the lush plantings in the garden. They take up little room yet provide a clean, clear path through the delphiniums, lupines, linaria, and roses.**

■ Cut pieces can be either regularly shaped pavers or bricks—that is, anything that comes in square, rectangular, or interlocking pieces and is laid close together to fill the space in the path completely. They are laid in patterns, some more intricate than others, and can take a great deal of time to do. The bricks or stones in formal walkways can be mortared for a really solid look.

■ Irregularly shaped materials include stepping-stones, flagstones, and other natural stone. They have a more informal look, leaving gaps between them that beg for some mat-forming plant to be tucked in (better that than letting the weeds take over). Irregular shapes also offer you the advantage of less site preparation. You can dig in each stepping-stone, or you can place the stones on top of the ground and then build up around them with soil and plants. If you choose the latter method, be sure that the transition (the beginning and the end of the walk) is not too abrupt, or you and everyone else will be tripping through the side garden.

■ Even before recycling was common-place, recycled concrete was used in the garden. Whole rockeries have been made from the stacked pieces, endless paths are laid with them, funky fountains are edged with them. Recycled concrete is so popular that you may have trouble finding enough for some projects, especially in spring, when garden-improvement fever hits everyone at the same time. Aside from taking a sledgehammer to a sidewalk on your own property (not the city's sidewalk), all you can do is scrounge, ask at demolition sites, and be on the lookout for someone else's home improvement project that may include getting rid of concrete.

Below: **This small garden has used a change of path materials—from formal brick to irregular stones—to mark a transition from pathway to open lawn.**

■ If the artist in you is just begging to come out when you think of making a new path, then you can create your own concrete stepping-stones and decorate them with shells, pottery shards, trinkets, costume

jewelry—just about anything that won't stick up above the surface too much. First, walk through the area and mark where your feet go; try this a couple of times until you're walking comfortably (no giant or mincing steps). Use quick-setting concrete, the kind that you can mix right in the hole if you want. Dig a hole the shape that you want the stepping-stone to be, pour in concrete, smooth over the top with a stiff piece of cardboard or a masonry trowel, and then place your decorations.

■ Gravel or crushed rock needs edging or it will gradually get walked away; you'll end up with a bare path and mounds of gravel on either side. It's not the best choice for a sloped path, because either it will tend to wash down the slope or you will slip around on it as you try to negotiate the rise or fall. With almost any loose material, you may find yourself tracking pieces of it out of the path because it sticks to your shoes.

■ Wood chips, in fairly regular sizes and without whole leaves and twigs, are available commercially. You can often get them free from an arborist, but the catch is that you must take their whole load, not just a little pile of it. An entire load can be several cubic yards, and that is a pile much larger than most small gardens can accommodate.

■ Bark is available in bags or bulk, and usually graded into sizes. The smallest size is really shredded, and will stick to everything as you walk through; the largest is too big to walk on comfortably.

■ Nutshells are available from some landscape supply companies, bagged at nurseries, or "from the source." In Oregon and Washington, hazelnut shells are sold by orchards. These shells are a rich brown color, last for several years, and have a more hollow-sounding crunch than gravel. Any tiny pieces of nuts left in the bags or piles are happy surprises for the squirrels.

A path of loose material is easier and faster to lay than one with fitted patterns of brick or stone. You simply build the frame and then fill in the middle, although it's still a good idea to delineate the path by digging down a couple of inches. Such paths can feel either formal or informal, depending on the materials used for filling and edging.

Gravel, with its rounded edges, tends to move more than sharp-edged material; more than a couple of inches of gravel, and you'll feel as though you're traveling through quicksand.

Color-coordinating your path is possible not only with pavers, where you can choose from shades of brick and gray, but also with colored gravel. Terra-cotta, pink, and blue-gray tones of gravel are all available, and different colors can even be mixed according to your taste. Buy the material in bulk or in bags from landscape supply companies.

Planting the Path

Below: **Organic path materials, such as the bark and wood chips here, give a woodland feel to the garden—a perfect complement to its dense planting of shade-loving lacecap hydrangeas.**

The irregular sizes of broken concrete lend themselves to a crazy-quilt approach to paths and patios. They provide lots of gardening spaces between them, and are perfect for plants that prefer a neutral or slightly alkaline soil, because the lime in the concrete sloughs off with age, and that raises the pH of the soil (a distinct advantage in the Pacific Northwest, where most soils are slightly acid). In the sun, grow

How Much Path Material Will You Need?

Solid path materials—pavers and such—are sold by dimension; loose materials are sold by the cubic foot or cubic yard. Figuring all this out can be daunting if you don't have a formula, and it's frustrating to end up with extra material that you can't find a place for in the small garden. Follow these steps to calculate just how much material you will need.

For solid materials:

■ Figure out the square footage of the area by multiplying the width times the length of the path.

■ If a particular stone is sold by weight, the landscape supply dealer will be able to convert your figure to approximately the right amount. It's always wise to make sure you can come back for a few more pieces of stone without having to buy another ton.

■ Bricks and formed pavers are often sold individually. Once you know the dimensions of the path and the size of the pavers, you'll be able to figure out how many you need.

For loose materials:

■ Loose material needs to be figured in three dimensions. Multiply the length times the width of the area times the depth you want.

■ Work all dimensions in feet to begin with (3 inches is 0.25 feet).

■ Divide the resulting figure by 27 to get cubic yards, which is how most of this material is sold (it's even listed that way on bags). For example: Your path is 20 feet long and 3 feet wide, and you want hazelnut shells 3 inches deep. That would be 20 x 3 x 0.25 = 15; that sum divided by 27 equals slightly more than half a cubic yard (0.55).

fragrant old-fashioned pinks *(Dianthus)* and mat-forming thymes (creeping, elfin, or woolly, or mother-of-thyme). Thymes take some foot traffic, as does Irish or Scotch moss *(Sagina subulata),* which forms tight cushions of green. Mat-forming thymes can be controlled in small spaces by trimming the edges back at the end of winter (which also neatens the plants).

Mat-forming plants for part shade include Corsican mint *(Mentha requienii),* which grows into a tight mass that is slightly springy to the touch (or step); it also gives off a light, minty fragrance. Less common, the species of New Zealand brass buttons *Cotula perpusilla* or *C. squalida* (also listed as *Leptinella squalida)* form a solid ground cover that, when examined closely, looks like tiny fern fronds. *Cotula* is evergreen, but turns a bronze tone in winter. Blue star creeper *(Pratia pedunculata)* is a popular stepping-stone plant that takes sun or part shade; it's covered in sky-blue flowers in early to midsummer. It's important to know that blue star creeper is semi-evergreen, another way of saying it looks ratty in winter; remember that if you're choosing a plant for a place you want to be green year-round.

Planting the Narrow Side Garden

Brushing by plants as you walk down a path, often releasing some scent from flowers or foliage, is a pleasant experience—one that connects you with the garden. But having to battle unyielding woody branches, being slapped in the face by wet leaves, or ducking and dodging hanging vines are not the experiences you're after. Neither do you want a stiff row of yew soldiers, standing at attention along the fence, or a flat, uninteresting carpet of ground cover and nothing else. A narrow area such as the side garden challenges us to look not just for narrow plants but for plants that can be layered to give a lush effect. Fortunately, in the Pacific Northwest, there is a wide palette of plants to provide color and texture year-round.

Selecting for Size and Shape

It's just no good trying to keep a wide plant skinny. You may think you can keep up with the pruning, but even if you do, the result is a sadly misshapen plant. So avoid plants that grow wide, and instead choose plants that normally have upright growth. *Enkianthus campanulatus*, a lovely shrub that can grow 15 feet high but only a few feet wide, would fit nicely along a path. The tiered growth of some *Mahonia* cultivars, such as *M. × media* 'Charity', 'Hope', and 'Winter Sun', gives a narrow space a layered look. These plants flower in fall and winter, and their yellow blooms brighten dark Northwest winters. They sucker, so you can cut whole stems back to the ground, leaving only enough stems to fit into the space. (It's necessary to keep these plants out of the way, because their leaflets are sharp and spiny, and getting stuck or scratched every time you walk by is one plant experience you don't need.) Look for more plant suggestions in the "Narrow Plants" list at the back of this book.

Below: **Small trees that are limbed up provide more room to underplant. Here, the underplanting includes a white masterwort (*Astrantia*), pink astilbe, hostas, and a variegated Solomon's seal (*Polygonatum odoratum* 'Variegatum').**

Tall shrubs can provide a canopy to shorter plants and ground covers. Layering plants in a narrow space gives you more space for plants in the small side garden. You can underplant tall, upright shrubs with a skirt of lower-growing shrubs and perennials, and below that you can use ground covers. This also means that the taller plants will be in more sun and the lower ones will be in shade. If you limb the shrubs up to about 4 feet, they will provide a wider canopy that you would be able to accommodate at face level. Vine maples *(Acer circinatum)*, larger cotoneasters, such as *C. divaricatus*, and even small trees such as the Japanese snowbell *(Styrax japonicum)* are all good candidates.

Limbing Up the Shrubs

In limbing up, work with the shrub's form, pruning off lower stems by cutting back to a main or thicker stem. If you are unsure whether you should remove a limb or not, take hold of it and shake. All the smaller branches and twigs that are attached will move, and you'll be more able to mentally "remove" the whole thing, seeing what will be left behind. Limbing up works particularly well with multistemmed shrubs, because they often add more visual interest than a single trunk does and because many shrubs have attractive bark. (Some, such as rhododendrons and *Pieris*, develop shredding bark after they reach a certain age.) Keep this in mind on nursery trips.

Left: **Under trees, use plants that are happy in part shade, such as this mix of purple-red coleus, ferns, and *Crocosmia*.**

Limbing up is especially helpful for shrubs that need some sun. They can be at the top of the "forest," catching rays, and creating a woodland environment below. The top layer of *Viburnum* x *burkwoodii* does well against an arbor or a fence, and has fragrant flowers in March. Underplant it with bold clumps of hostas, such as *Hosta sieboldiana* 'Elegans', which can grow to 3 feet high and 4 feet across. Although hostas die back in winter, they have an impressive presence spring to fall. Finish the garden floor with a carpet of the evergreen Allegheny spurge *(Pachysandra procumbens)*. Spring bulbs and woodland flowers such as the yellow Welsh poppy *(Meconopsis cambrica)* add a colorful spark. Layering gives you something of interest along the path all year long.

Sun in the Side Garden

The top layer of plants may be the only ones that get sun. Small side gardens are the parts of your garden most likely to be shady because of buildings blocking the light. Since the angle of the sun during the day changes through the year, a spot that was sunny just a few weeks before can suddenly become shady in the morning. Trees overhead, large conifers across the alley or two gardens down, and, of course, the solid shade from the house and other buildings all do their part to rob the side garden of light. Fortunately, deciduous trees are usually less dense than conifers; sunlight can sneak through the layers of leaves to land on plants below at various times through the day as the sun travels across the sky.

Remember that from May until August, the path of the sun will be more or less directly overhead—peaking, of course, on the summer solstice (June 21), the longest day of the year, when it seems that in the Northwest, the sun doesn't set until about 11 P.M. Also note that in winter, whatever weak sunshine is around is low in the Northwest sky. It's a good thing that plants don't do a lot of photosynthesizing in winter.

Space and sun are the two overriding factors in the side garden. Take advantage of the sun where it appears—one end of the side garden usually will be sunnier than the middle or the other end. Like a stopped clock that is right twice a day, shady side gardens do get sun, most often in the morning and/or afternoon, when the light finds a direct path between houses, trees, or office buildings. Within the side garden, after carefully analyzing how much sun is there, choose plants that do well in low light or in part shade, depending on the conditions you've found. Shrubs and perennials that are native to the understory of forests are good candidates for shade.

Water and the Side Garden

Often, understory plants are accustomed to less water than you might imagine. We all picture forests as being damp places, but rainfall is taken up in many ways before smaller understory plants can receive any of it. The tree canopy intercepts some rain, and by the time the water hits the ground the tree roots may take up a lot of it. The ground itself, although fortunately covered with a thick layer of decaying plant litter that helps the soil retain moisture, is filled with roots, all vying for what moisture does get there.

If your side garden is pure sun—concrete between house and fence—you can line one side or another with containers that hold vines and sun-loving mounding plants such as colorful sedums (*Sedum* 'Vera Jameson' grows to 1 foot and has dark-red leaves and deep-pink flower heads). If you don't want to attach trellises directly to the wall or fence, you can set them out a few inches and attach them with eye screws. A rose that grows long stems even though it may not be considered a climber can be used on a trellis in a narrow place. *Rosa moyesii* 'Geranium', with single, deep pink-red flowers and bottle-shaped hips, grows to 10 feet without getting bushy; with its long canes secured, it would display flowers and hips nicely.

The Other Side Garden

If you have room for a path on one side of the house, you may have nothing but a thin strip of land on the other side. You don't use this side of the garden because it's too narrow to walk through; you may not even see it. It's easy to let the weeds and grass take over. But your neighbor sees it, and when you catch the occasional glimpse, you're shocked at the state of things.

Plant easy-care ground covers, and let annuals reseed in areas you can't reach. Mat-forming ground covers need little maintenance. In the sun, use creeping thyme; in the shade, *Cotula*. Sprinkle seeds or plant annuals that will reseed year after year. You may need to do a small amount of winter cleanup. When you pull the dead annuals out, remember to sprinkle the seeds out so that you'll get a new crop next year. Good annuals for sun include feverfew, Shirley poppies, cosmos, *Linaria purpurea*, and *Cleome*. Annuals for part shade include Johnny-jump-up, Welsh poppy *(Meconopsis cambrica)*, and foxgloves. Once established, old-fashioned bearded iris do well in the sun. They need less water in summer than in winter, and so fit with our Northwest climate.

You Light Up My Life: Variegated Plants

You don't need electricity to turn on the lights in the garden.
Plants that are splashed and edged in gold or silver can illumi-
nate dark corners and make sunny spots even brighter.
Variegated plants make a valuable addition to small gardens in
the gray, overcast skies of the Northwest fall and winter (and
spring). Variegated plants show up best when mixed with non-
variegated ones.

Variegation in plants usually is caused by a mutation—one
branch on a green plant grows white-and-green leaves.
(Occasionally, a virus causes foliage to be variegated, and this is
difficult to perpetuate.) Once in a while, variegation is a normal
part of plant makeup, and in this case the characteristic is
passed down from generation to generation; the variegation will
come true from seed, as it does in the annual *Euphorbia marginata* (snow on the mountain). Even more occasionally, variegation can be caused by herbicide damage or mineral-deficient
soils; obviously, those causes are transient.

The majority of the variegated plants available to gardeners
are from mutations. Here, normally green plants exhibit yellow or
white (sometimes pink or shades of green) markings on the
leaves of perhaps just one stem. These nongreen areas either
lack chlorophyll or have much less than the green areas. A lack
of chlorophyll (the impetus for cell division and therefore growth)
means that the variegated stem doesn't grow as fast or as big
as the rest of the plant.

When the strange foliage is noticed (in someone's garden, in a
nursery or at a grower's, or out in nature), and if it's a remarkably
attractive variegation (although the beauty of variegation is a
matter of opinion), some alert plantsman or plantswoman will
take cuttings from that branch. These cuttings are rooted and

grown on into bigger plants, which we then buy at nurseries. Because these plants are vegetatively propagated, the unusual colors and patterns in the leaves will not occur on plants grown from seed. Once in a while, a variegated plant will produce non-variegated (that is, all green) branches; such stems are said to have reverted. Gardeners keep an eye out for this occurrence and prune out the reversion; otherwise, the more vigorous green foliage may overtake the rest of the plant.

For some examples, see the "Variegated Plants" list at the back of this book.

Below: **Plants with variegated foliage, such as this snow-on-the-mountain (Euphorbia marginata), brighten up the garden even when no showy flowers are present.**

Chapter Four

- **Fencing the Small Back Garden**

- **Hedges for the Small Garden**

- **Have a Seat**

- **The Small Lawn**

- **Hiding the Unsightly Essentials**

- **Elegant Espalier for Walls and Fences**

- **The Neighbor's Weeds**

Left: **A back garden—even a small one—can provide sanctuary and privacy to the gardener, no matter what lies just beyond the gate.**

The Back Garden

It's your private place, your oasis, your escape from the busyness of life. But escaping to your back-garden retreat may be difficult if you feel peering eyes from neighbors, alley traffic, and the garbage truck. In order to get a bit of privacy, many gardeners are willing to barricade themselves behind tall fences and towering hedges, which can take up a good bit of space. Then where is the room for the rest of the garden, let alone the barbecue and a place to sit?

Your entrance to the back garden may be through a gate from the side garden or alley, through the garage, or out the back door. Next door could be 6 feet away; garbage trucks may rattle down the alley weekly. Your neighbor might have one of those decks on stilts so that

How to Borrow Views

Make your small garden larger without adding a square foot of property by borrowing the scenery around you. Whether it's a view of downtown Seattle, Mount Rainier, or Vancouver's English Bay, plants in just the right places can frame a view beyond your property, and draw your attention to it. If your garden is already full of mature plants, you need to look around and visualize what is behind that large hedge of yours. Is it something you want to see? If lowering the hedge will keep your privacy yet allow you to have a view of the city or mountains, then it would be worth it to renovate (or even replace) the hedge. Starting from scratch, you can pick and choose which fabulous views you want to borrow.

To keep it simple, frame a borrowed view with plants that won't grow so wide or high that they eventually block the special sight (and leave you with yet another maintenance job). Your choice of plants and placement will depend on where you most often sit or stand to see the view. If you look out the kitchen window, use a row of *Choisya ternata* (Mexican orange), an evergreen shrub that won't grow over 5 feet. On each end of the frame, plant a narrow conical evergreen. Otherwise, you will end up replacing plants or trying to maintain a size and shape for which that tree or shrub isn't suited.

If the view you borrow is seen from only one place in the garden, make it a dramatic moment by planting a tall-but-narrow yew that you must walk around for the site to be suddenly revealed.

he can get a view of Mount Baker or Mount Hood; it looms over your back garden, exposing all of your activities to his gaze. You may want a little piece of lawn for your Adirondack chair. And the kids would love a sandbox.

The small back garden is a multipurpose room. It's an idyllic scene at the best of times, but one that can be beset with small, nagging problems. For example, it's difficult to position that Adirondack where you can enjoy a nice view for your quiet time, if everywhere you look is "not the best angle." Small gardens often mean living in close quarters with the everyday business of modern urban living. So one of the first decisions to make is how much of an escape you want your back garden to be.

Public or Private?

Is your back garden public or private? You may live out of the back of your house. For some people, the back door and garden can become almost like a front porch, especially if your house is on a busy street. If your neighbors feel the same way, the back garden can have as much of a community feel as the front stoop. You may look out the back door the same way someone else walks out onto the front porch to see who is coming up the neighbor's steps. It's a place to visit, to be open to hellos over the fence. After all, it's hard to ignore someone when she is standing 15 feet away, whether or not there's a fence between you.

If you choose, you can create a neighborly back garden with shared space by knocking down fences and opening hedges. You may even want to develop a garden co-op, where you can share the sunniest parts of both properties in order to have a larger vegetable garden.

Many people, however, have enough of public display in front. Usually, gardeners on small properties are looking for ways to escape, not join, the crowd. And that means taller hedges and fences—our defense against the constant intrusions of life.

Fencing the Small Back Garden

Some people may like the idea of no fences, where several neighbors' gardens merge into one. And in some places, this is just the ticket. Where a group of houses is built as a community, with only a scrap of land each, going in together on a garden makes great sense. We are, however, more used to rows of separate houses, each with its own private garden. In this case, the fence is a statement of purpose: This is where I would like some peace and quiet, with no one using my garden as a public path. Fences can help make it easier to be friendly because you aren't constantly concerned about the invisible strip of land that separates you from your neighbor. The lines are clearly drawn, and if your color scheme of yellow and orange doesn't suit his shades of pink, no one will be able to see. Good fences can indeed make good neighbors.

If there is an existing fence between you and the property next door, find out who built it. The style may not be your favorite, but if the fence was put up by the neighbor, then it isn't a good idea for you to tear it down. If there is no fence and you plan to build one, it only makes good sense for you to at least mention it to your neighbor, who may be relieved that she will no longer have to look at the back side of your compost bin.

Below: **Give plants an opening—as this openwork fence does—and they will grow through, the foliage softening the hard lines of lumber.**

Fence Styles

■ A picket fence lends a cottage look. Picket fences leave you space in the small garden, because you can see over and through them. And any fence with see-through gaps is good for holding up climbing or rambling roses. You can let vines wander in and out of the pickets. Picket-fence lengths are normally 3 feet high; some have a formal cutout at the top, while others are flat-topped. Buy sections of picket fence, or buy the wood and do it yourself. With a custom-made picket fence, you can choose pieces as small as 1 inch by 1 inch instead of the standard 3- to 4-inch width. For a clean, no-nonsense look, run a section of evenly spaced flat pickets that are all the same height. For a more romantic look, use a section of pickets that are tall at the posts and dip down toward the middle, creating a swag.

■ The neat, tight arrangement of a 5- or 6-foot-high wooden fence (with or without a formal cap at the top) is a no-nonsense privacy statement. In the Northwest, Western red cedar is a popular choice, one that can be stained or left to weather to gray. If you want a fence taller than 5 feet, check first to see whether your city has height restrictions on fences.

■ A fence that is solid up to 5 feet and then opens to a peekaboo cutout pattern along the top foot has a slightly more open feel, giving the impression that you want privacy but you don't mind an admiring glance from a passerby. The openwork lets in more light, and creates a twining place for vines.

■ Bamboo fences are not as common as cedar fencing, but the material is becoming more popular. Bamboo now comes in many different styles, some with openwork like lattice, others solid. It's a (quickly) renewable resource, and is long lasting.

■ If you need only a section of fence as a short screen or to create a separate space, you will still have to do some installation. The fence/screen will need to be anchored or it will blow over in the wind (and maybe take out some plants on its way). If it's a short picket fence that doesn't support anything, you don't have to dig a posthole and pour concrete in, but you will have to stabilize the ends with posts that are set snugly several inches into the soil. Even long-lasting Western red cedar, when it's in contact with soil, will eventually rot. To slow this inevitable decay, use a Northwest Native American technique: char the end of the post that will go into the soil.

Fence Microclimates

Fences change the sun-and-shade pattern of the garden, so installing one may change your plant selection. In the small garden the difference between a sunny area and a shady one is sometimes quite dramatic because of the shade from a tall fence or nearby building. That is accentuated in the Northwest, where late fall through early spring brings the sun in at such a low point in the sky that sometimes you barely notice it.

Fences create microclimates by trapping sunlight or excluding it. A solid fence built on a south property line will block some morning and afternoon light—and maybe even some midday light in winter, when the sun is so low in the sky. Because some of the light is gone anyway, it's best to keep the area under shrubs clear. Limb tall shrubs up to 3 or 4 feet so that it doesn't seem so dark and dank underneath. Rake out excess leaves and trash regularly (the area is like a magnet). You'll be able to use woodland plants to good effect here, as the overhead shrubs will let just enough light in, and little of it will be direct or sustained. (Some evergreen shrubs, however, such as evergreen *Camellia japonica*, are just too dense to let in light.)

A solid fence on the north side of your property creates a different environment. It captures the sun's warmth against its south face, which it shows to you. A wall of brick or stone adds extra warmth because it absorbs heat from the sun, which it then radiates. This means not only that it will be hotter during the day but that the warmth will linger after the sun goes down, as the wall releases the stored heat.

Any fence on the north side of your garden gives you an opportunity to use shrubs and perennials that are marginally hardy, or that do best in more sun and heat than we can usually muster. The wall provides

protection from harsh winds, too. African daisies (*Osteospermum* spp.) grow to be shrubby perennials with protection and heat; they are available with either all-green or variegated foliage, and the flowers may be white, lavender, or sometimes two-toned. New Zealand flax *(Phormium)* is another plant in need of protection and heat. Its swordlike leaves contrast well with mounds of flowers. *Phormium* 'Flamingo' has pink and apricot tones to the leaves; 'Dusky Chief' is wine-red, and grows up to 5 feet. When you plan this warm area, be sure to take into account buildings that may block sunlight (see "How to Follow the Sun" in Chapter One).

A fence on the east side of your property, if it's unobstructed by buildings or dense evergreens, will receive, in effect, full sun. In contrast, plants along a fence on the west side of your property will get relief from hot afternoon sun, so this would be the perfect place for those plants that need part shade.

Fences as Supports for Plants

Above: **Heat-loving plants such as cannas and dahlias are best used in the sunniest parts of the garden, such as against a south-facing wall.**

Decorate the fence with plants. You aren't limited to growing shrubs or woody perennials in front of a fence. Vines are perfect fence companions; most of them need some sort of support, and sometimes the supports can be part of the ornament.

■ A section of lattice (a common size is 4 feet by 8 feet) nailed into the fence not only helps hold up a plant, it also adds depth to the fence; this is another way to make the small garden seem bigger through the optical illusion of depth. You can frame the lattice if you want (specially cut wood pieces are available from the lumber store) or leave its edges open for a more informal look.

■ Window-screen mesh or hardware cloth can also be made into vine support. Take a section, spray-paint it brown or black, and frame it with 1-inch-by-1-inch wood strips that have been stained brown. The color effect of the screen/trellis is subtle; it blends into the fence and the vine covers it, yet even standing alone it has a classy effect. Window screening has tiny holes, so to grow a clematis on it you'll need to add projections, such as nails, that the leaf stems can coil around (or use hardware cloth with bigger holes). Climbing roses would need to be tied up to the projections, as for an espaliered shrub, but vines such as sweet peas, which use tendrils to climb, could easily work their way into the hardware cloth.

■ Old windows, the kind with wood-divided, separate panes, provide a sense of depth to the garden, too. These treasures have a lot of character. Check around at junk stores or salvage yards (or you may even find a couple in your basement or garage). Just remove the glass, sand down the flaking paint (or leave it for the old-farmhouse look, but remember that if it's more than 20 years old it may be lead-based), and attach them to a fence. An annual purple-flowered morning glory vine or a bright orange nasturtium can grow up through and out of the empty panes, making you wonder whether you are looking out at the flowers or they are looking in at you.

■ Use a section of chain-link fence, 2 feet wide and as tall as your fence, for a low-cost vine support with no construction needed. Spray-paint

Fuzzy Borders

Solid walls and fences stop the eye, and there's no mistaking the end of a garden when you see the alley or a parked car. But designers use tricks to make us think that there is no property line, or at least to make it look that way. These techniques can be useful in the small garden. If you "hide" the fence and gate with a screen of plants, your eye is deceived into thinking that the garden doesn't stop 20 feet away. It may only be the path to the trash or the alley, but if you screen it off with a trellis and allow a billowing plant to cover the support, the steps appear to turn a corner and go . . . how far? It's difficult to tell, even though stepping-stones or a marked path make it evident that there is more. The trellis hides the borders of your garden.

If the spot is sunny, plant a potato vine, *Solanum crispum* 'Glasnevin', which has purple-blue flowers with yellow centers and blooms over a long period in the summer. The flowers look like the blooms of a potato or tomato (with good reason, because they are in the same genus). It's a plant that is perfectly hardy in most of the Pacific Northwest, except on high ridges, where it may be cut to the ground in a freeze. Sometimes described as a Lax shrub, the plant will need tying up, but offers a soft, floating form that belies the flat surface of the trellis. Vary the heights and textures of plants that hide the entire length of the back fence and stagger the plantings—some up against the fence, others out a few feet. This, too, will help disguise the end of the garden. A good choice for part shade would be the Lax shrub *Disanthus cercidifolius*, which has heart-shaped leaves and good fall color.

the chain link a neutral color that will blend in, and hang it from cup hooks at the top of the fence or wall. This will give vines with tendrils or coiling leaf stems something substantial to twine around.

Hedges for the Small Garden

A green, living wall seems less confrontational than a tall fence; it's a softer way of maintaining your privacy. For centuries, hedges have made it easy to see what belongs where. In the English countryside, hedgerows are used. Hedgerows are made up of various shrubs and trees that form a thicket—sort of the green equivalent of a city's mixed-use housing. They keep livestock in, while hosting a thriving community of birds and small animals by providing food and cover. In formal English gardens, huge hedges of black-green yew, always sheared so smooth they look like a solid surface, form boundaries. Large estates have room for a hedge 20 feet high and as wide; in a small garden, there would be no garden left.

Right: **Tall blue** *Campanula lactiflora* **stands out against a hedge of evergreen English holly.**

Below: **Evergreen huckleberry** *(Vaccinium ovatum)* **makes a fine informal hedge to about 4 feet high, with the added benefit of edible fruit for you or the birds.**

Hedges can give a "finished" look to a formal setting or be a part of the informal cottage look. They can do more than keep something out or in: they can provide a backdrop to your garden. Flowers, variegated foliage, and contrasting textures of both leaf and flower stand out well against a uniform canvas. An evergreen hedge shows off flowers better if it is planted to the north of the flowers so that they have the sun shining directly on them rather than from behind the hedge.

Tall or Short?

Not all hedges need to be tall and solid. Hedges just 2 or 3 feet high can delineate the lines of a garden, speaking softly of boundaries without blocking areas completely. This element has been used to perfection in herb and kitchen gardens, where lavender, boxwood *(Buxus)*, or germander *(Teucrium)* is often grown as the frame for lettuce, broccoli, and corn. Use a low border hedge when you want to make a statement of possession but still want to see what's on the other side.

When you plan for a view-blocking hedge, take into consideration what you do and don't want to see. You may indeed need a wall of green running the entire length of the back property line or along the side from front walk to alley. Or you may have just one particular sight that you don't want to see, or one particular spot from which you don't want to be seen. Walk through the garden on your usual

paths, sit down in all the normal places, and look around from each. If only one or two spots need "covering," it would be a waste of your precious garden space to plant a 20-foot-long hedge. One dark yew or a group of three strategically placed, narrow-growing conifers can effectively block the sight of the neighbor's back door from your favorite garden seat, while maintaining your view of the city skyline, a lake, or a particularly striking oak tree four doors down.

Evergreen or Deciduous?

Decide whether you want a deciduous or an evergreen hedge. We automatically think that hedges have to be evergreen, because who wants to see through them in winter? Ask yourself: Who would see through them in winter? It could be that you are screening something off that bothers you only when you are barbecuing in summer. If seasonal blockage is all you need, a deciduous hedge offers that, and it also lets the sun shine in so that you can plant a carpet of bulbs beneath for early bloom.

Above: **A row of just three narrow-growing evergreens can screen a particular view and even create more room—by dividing the garden without actually walling a section off. You can't see through the screen, but you can easily walk around it and be in a different space.**

Don't dismiss the idea of a country hedgerow even in the small garden. A mix of evergreen and deciduous shrubs offers interest in all seasons while also providing some privacy. If you choose some berried shrubs to interplant with the evergreens, you'll be providing cover and food for city wildlife. For more ideas on plants to use in hedges, see the "Hedges" plant list at the back of this book.

Conifer or Broadleaf Evergreen?

If you want an evergreen hedge, decide between conifers or broadleaf evergreens. To most Northwesterners, the term "evergreen" is practically synonymous with the term "conifer"; we think of cedars, Douglas firs, spruces, and so on. But there are a number of broadleaf evergreens to choose from. (A broadleaf evergreen is any tree or shrub that keeps its leaves all winter long but is not a conifer.) The most common broadleaf evergreen plants used for hedges in the Northwest (not the best, just the most common) are English laurel *(Prunus lauro-cerasus)*, Portuguese laurel *(P. lusitanica),* and photinia (*Photinia* × *fraseri,* sometimes called "red tip" for the color of its new growth). All three have leaves that are about 2 to 3 inches across and 4 to 6 inches long. They quickly form glossy green walls, growing to 6 feet in just a couple of years.

These broadleaf evergreens all take shearing well, which is a good thing, because you'll have to do it often—they are, normally, 30-foot trees. However, although they recover well from the hedge shears, they may look tattered at first. That's because they "break from wood," meaning that they possess leaf buds that are buried underneath the bark on woody stems (these are called adventitous buds). If the stem or branch is cut, hormones are released that break these buds into growth, and new leaves grow straight out of solid wood.

Conifers are classic hedge plants, so much so that there are dozens from which to choose. A fast-growing choice is the Leyland cypress (× *Cupressocyparis leylandii*), a plant about which it was once said that its best attribute is that it grows quickly. But many conifers aren't as accommodating as broadleaf English laurel—they won't break from wood. That is why it's important to keep up maintenance on a conifer hedge. Light shearing (that is, pruning that does not go back into wood) once or twice a year, cutting off some but not all green growth, is desirable. Drastic cutting that goes back into wood will result in holes in the hedge—woody gaps that won't fill up again.

Planting and Maintaining Hedges

Hedges that are well-chosen, well-planted, and well-maintained can last for decades. Follow these tips for a good hedge:

■ Depending on the particular species and cultivar, you can set plants out anywhere from 18 to 35 inches apart. Sometimes the density of planting is determined by how much money you have to spend and how quickly you want the hedge to fill in.

■ Plant to the depth you would any shrub or tree; that is, keep the trunk at the same level as, or slightly higher than, it was in the container.

A balled-and-burlapped plant has the root ball wrapped up and tied, but once you've pulled the burlap away from the trunk, you should still be able to figure out how deep to plant. Take a close look at the base of the trunk—there should be a slight flare where trunk joins crown (where the root structure begins). Don't cover up the flare with soil; in fact, set the plant so that the flare is a couple of inches above soil level.

■ As with any woody plant, either amend the soil in a large area (the entire row and several feet to either side) or (this is easier) mulch after planting with good-quality compost. The one thing that kills new hedges more often than anything else is lack of water. Woody plants need regular water until they are established—and that's not just to the end of the first year, it means for at least two successive summers.

■ And speaking of water, hedges are known for sucking up water to the detriment of nearby plants, just as tree roots do. This may affect your plant selection for the planting area just in front of the hedge. Mulch, again, comes to the rescue: a good layer of compost in the bed will help maintain moisture.

Pruning Hedges

■ Conifers chosen for their narrow growth habit, and especially those with a maximum height of 10 to 12 feet, can be left untended—they already have a neat appearance.

■ Other conifers, and all broadleaf evergreens, especially those with dense and twiggy growth such as boxwood, need to be sheared in a wedge shape, slightly broader at the base than at the top. This exposes as much of the plant as possible to sunlight, encouraging good, leafy growth. Formal shapes such as this wedge are easier to maintain with broadleaf evergreens that have small leaves, such as boxwood.

■ An alternative to shearing is to prune plants selectively, cutting the tallest stems down to the first joint of another stem. This is done by reaching down inside the plant, not just cutting the stem off and leaving a stub. Selective pruning works exceptionally well with stiffly upright shrubs such as holly olive *(Osmanthus heterophyllus)* and even yew *(Taxus)*; it produces a fairly uniform hedge without creating the usual interior space full of dead twigs.

Gaps in Hedges

Inevitably, just as your box hedge has gained some girth and substance, the plant right smack in the middle of the row starts to look peaked. You know its time is near, and you don't know what you're going to do with the hole that's left. If you were the owner of a large garden, you would have room for one or more "nursery beds." These are areas out of view where you can hold extra hedge plants (bought at the same time, so that, when they are used as replacements, they'll be approximately the same size); extra plants for which you haven't found a place; and small plants, often propagated from cuttings or layering, that are not yet big enough for the garden. There is no such luxury in the small garden, so plan ahead when you install the hedge. Ask the nursery whether this is a common variety you're choosing, whether it's hard to get, and whether it comes in a larger size than you are buying (if you're buying 1-gallon containers now, ask whether you'll be able to buy a 5-gallon size in five years). The answers may affect your choice. Sometimes when a hedge plant dies, though, you need to be creative. That gap in the hedge could be just the place for a piece of garden art or a new birdbath.

Out-of-Control Hedges

What if you have a hedge that's already out of control—can it be saved? The question goes back to those adventitious buds. A huge laurel hedge can be cut down to 6 inches from the ground and it will—eventually—grow back, bushier than ever, although this will take years. A laurel hedge that's too wide can be cut back on one side (and often is—sometimes by neighbors who take drastic action against what they see as invasive plants), leaving bare wood that makes it look like the back of a stage set. That, too, will sprout again. An arborvitae hedge *(Thuja occidentalis*, another popular choice for a coniferous screen) will not come back from stumps. In many cases of drastic renovation, it's better to rethink the whole hedge thing.

Barrier Hedges

Plants that you use to keep people and animals out of your garden (as opposed to keeping your livestock in, unless you have a couple of chickens running around) are usually pretty to look at but painful to encounter. Prickly or thorny plants can be just as good as a lock and key, and many can be trimmed into formal hedges. (There's a job you might want to hire out.) *Rugosa* roses will grow into a prickly mass, and they have the added benefit of fragrant flowers in summer and showy red hips in fall, but they look best when left free-form. Barberries (*Berberis* spp.) have thorns in threes that appear just under the leaf; they can be trimmed for a hedge. In the small garden, be careful about where you plant a barrier hedge. Don't plant one in an area that needs to be accessed by you or anyone else (the meter reader, for example).

Have a Seat

Above: **English holly (*Ilex aquifolium)* is a borderline pest plant, but it accepts shearing well (which keeps it to a manageable size), and its prickly leaves make it a dandy barrier hedge.**

Even without the luxury of an acre and winding paths that lead to the cutting garden (which is never viewed directly), you can still find places in the small garden for a bench or chair. Intimate seating is the hallmark of the small garden—if we can't do it well, who can?

The garden bench can be a focal point at the end of a path: an elegant English teakwood seat with pots of apple blossom–pink pelargoniums on either side and pale blue love-in-a-mist creating an airy mass beneath the seat (the pastels, remember, will recede visually, making the path look longer and the garden bigger). Or you can hide from view by placing a bench and a small table to hold drinks around a corner or under a wide arbor with climbing roses growing up and over it.

The sky's the limit when it comes to style selection for the garden bench. Besides the classic teak bench, you can find one-of-a-kind funky seats made from recycled barn wood or woven out of willow; plastic benches (often made from recycled materials) that look like wood; and sleek, modern styles. Or stick with the traditional Northwest look and choose Western red cedar.

The style of the bench, although of great concern, isn't as important as what you intend to do with it. Is your garden bench for looking at or for sitting on? Many gardeners prefer to have a lovely arrangement of bench and pots without ever a thought of actually sitting on it. Other gardeners may intend to sit on it, but when all is said and done, more time is spent selecting the spot for the bench so that the bench, rather than the view, looks nice. When you actually go to sit on it, you find you're staring at your neighbor's back door or the wall of your garage.

Below: **Choose the most inviting spot in the garden for chairs or benches. The view from this small seating area, against the side hedge, takes in the entire back garden.**

If you do intend to use your bench and not just view it, take a stool out to the garden with you and try out every conceivable space the bench might go (the stool will be much easier to move around than the actual bench). When you find a good viewing point, leave the stool, go inside, and look out the window to see if it looks as good from inside as it does from outside. Many an artful photograph has been taken of a single chair in the garden. But, in reality, a single chair looks lonely. Create a grouping that makes it look like you're ready for company: group two chairs together with a tiny table between them or three chairs around a low, round table.

And here's a tip for the gardener who is also space-conscious indoors. During our Northwest winter, few days are fit for sitting outdoors. So, at the end of the season, clean up your bench or chairs and find a place for them inside. Not only will you add seating space for winter entertaining, you'll be bringing a bit of the garden indoors with you.

The Small Lawn

Many gardeners strike a balance that they're happy with between lawn area and ornamental plants, while others like to dig up every blade of grass to make room for more roses. As tight as space is, the small garden is quite capable of incorporating a small lawn as long as the lawn's requirements and the gardener's tolerance are taken into consideration. And even a small lawn can add a cooling effect in a full-sun garden, as well as providing something soft to walk on in bare feet.

■ Shade mixes are available for lawns, but they work only so far. If your lawn doesn't receive at least a half-day of sun, you may end up with a moss garden. We should consider moss our friend in the Northwest; it grows in shady, damp, poorly drained conditions, where other things won't.

Below: **A patch of lawn is a cool contrast to flowers and shrubs, setting off their colors and forms**.

■ Design your small lawn so that it has straight edges or the very broadest of curves. It will be easier to mow and edge, and you can use the rounded forms of perennials and low shrubs to soften any hard lines.

■ Separate ornamental (or vegetable) beds from the grass by at least 6 inches for ease of maintenance and a cleaner look. Dig a shallow, dry moat between the two, but don't leave it bare or grass will grow back. Fill the moat with rocks (conveniently dug out from the garden—or purchased if necessary). You'll have an easier time seeing the boundary and plucking out what shouldn't be there. If the moat is just below the level of the lawn, you can mow right over it.

■ Use edging, but remember that if it sticks up, you'll have to use two tools to cut the grass—a lawn mower and an edger. Edging materials include long strips of brown plastic; sections of molded concrete finished off with scalloped tops; decorative antique-looking rusted iron pieces to lend a Victorian style; and bricks, which can be laid at an angle, long side up, to form a pinked edge. Bricks can also be laid flat, three or four wide. Sinking them level with the soil will help keep the grass from creeping into the beds.

An Alternative to Grass

There is an alternative to the all-grass lawn. You may find that keeping up with your small lawn of traditional turf is more work than it's worth—fertilizing twice a year, mowing once a week, and watering incessantly. Sounds like fun, no? There is now an alternative to the needy lawn, and that is a seed mix generally referred to as eco-turf. The mix has some grass seed, plus seeds of various broadleaf plants including yarrow, English daisy, and clover. Studies have shown that you can mow less often (maintaining a height of 2 inches) and water less often (about an inch and a half once a month in summer).

Eco-lawns don't need herbicide applications (indeed, herbicides would kill off some of the plants), which leaves you, your children, and your pets able to wander about barefoot without worrying about what you might pick up. In the Pacific Northwest, where we often give up watering lawns come summer, the eco-turf lawn stands out as having some green to it, as compared to conventional grass lawns that turn completely brown. Several companies sell this kind of seed mix, but almost any nursery should be able to point you to the correct shelf when you ask about it.

Hiding the Unsightly Essentials

In the small garden, there doesn't seem to be anywhere to put anything. Garbage, recycling, compost—our modern life abounds with necessities that take up valuable garden space. And then there is the garage—yours or the neighbors'—that shows a solid, blank wall to the garden.

The Garage Wall

Consider the blank wall of a garage as an opportunity. It's another way to add plants to the small garden. Vines, tall shrubs, sun-loving perennials (if the garage faces south or west), or woodland plants (if it faces north or east), singly or in combinations, can help draw the eye away from the blank wall, providing interest and depth. Many beautiful artist-designed trellises can be found at good nurseries and garden shops. (You may even find one that you want to display on its own, without a plant.)

Give yourself and your garage up to a beautiful, vigorous vine if you dare. This is just the place to grow a *Clematis montana* var. *rubens* 'Elizabeth' or one of the white cultivars such as *C. montana* 'Alexander'. The evergreen clematis, *C. armandii*, which blooms in March and April, has sprays of small white, starry flowers (pink in the cultivar 'Apple Blossom'). All of these vines are fragrant.

If the garage wall is yours, you can feel free to use mortar screws or eyebolts to attach supports for vines. Vines that need no support, such as the creepers (*Parthenocissus* spp.), can attach their suction pads to your paint with impunity, because you will be the one to decide when and how to repaint the wall.

If it's your neighbor's garage, a little delicacy is in order. First of all, find out exactly where the property line is, so that you aren't accused of overstepping your bounds. On that line or at least a foot away from the garage wall, you can install a trellis, either building it yourself or buying one ready-made.

Trellises range from 2 feet to 6 feet wide; a row of three small ones would fill up even more room than one large one, because you can leave small gaps between them. Some you can stick right into the ground, and others you may want to reinforce by digging postholes and using a quick-setting concrete. You may be able to dig holes and insert PVC piping in a diameter slightly larger than the stakes of the trellis. This will allow you to pick up and move the trellis whenever you need to (and also makes it easier to repaint).

Exposure dictates plant choice. A blank garage wall that faces south or west captures sun, heating up in the afternoon and staying warm as the surrounding air cools off. This is a wonderful place for espaliered fruit such as grapes, and also for half-hardy plants, such as one of the taller *Abutilon* cultivars. Abutilons, commonly known as flowering maples because of their leaf shape, have been grown for ages as conservatory plants, yet they grow well outdoors from spring through fall. Their bell-shaped flowers, which look like crepe paper, come in shades of yellow ('Moonchimes'), red ('Vesuvius'), and apricot ('Kentish Belle'), and would show up well against a wall of a contrasting color.

Evergreen firethorn *(Pyracantha coccinea)* grows into a wide shrub, but trained against a garage wall or fence it is manageable and displays showy orange-red fruit against dark green leaves all through the winter (until, when the fruit is at last ripe enough, the robins feast on it). 'Fiery Cascade' and 'Lowboy' are just two of many cultivars available.

If your garage wall gets morning sun, that can be just as valuable for you as for your plants. This could be the right spot for a small table and two chairs, where you can drink your coffee and watch the garden day begin in relative warmth, even on a chilly spring morning. Shrubs that take part shade, such as the fragrant and semi-evergreen *Viburnum* x *burkwoodi* or the variegated half vine, half shrub x *Fatshedera lizei* 'Media-Picta', are suited for half-day shade. Or put a pot of scarlet ivy geranium on the table, and the delicate annual canary-bird vine *Tropaeolum peregrinum* with its yellow flowers beside you on a trellis, and you'll want the morning to go on and on.

Garbage Bins and Toolsheds

Before you start constructing screens to hide garbage bins or toolsheds, think first about the angle from which you need to do the screening. You may not care that people walking down the alley can see the garbage can, as long as you don't have to look at it from the kitchen window. Don't box off more than you need to, or you'll make it difficult for yourself to drag the bins out.

To disguise bins and utilitarian toolsheds, build a section of framed lattice and let a small vine do the decorating. Lattice pieces come precut, usually 4 feet by 8 feet. You can buy already-cut framing for them and do it yourself. You can also buy fence sections, solid on the bottom and lattice on the top. Sweet autumn clematis *(Clematis paniculata)* is an evergreen vine that could cover the lattice within a season or two (and then it'll look for something else to hold onto, so keep an eye on it). It takes part shade. As with all vines, you may need to guide its stems where you want them to go, instead of letting them wander off into the Japanese maple next door. Clematis stems can be brittle, so proceed with care.

Below: **This broomhead farmer and blooming** *Ligularia stenocephala* **'The Rocket' distract us from wondering what lies ahead.**

Plant small shrubs at the base of an enclosure. Some plants that we think of as ground covers will climb, or at least grow up against, a vertical surface. Rock cotoneaster *(Cotoneaster horizontalis)* is a good example: its stems will grow several feet up a wall, revealing a herringbone pattern in winter when the leaves are gone and the red berries remain. Evergreen *Euonymus fortunei* 'Emerald 'n' Gold' (with yellow variegation) or 'Emerald Gaiety' (with white variegation) will also "climb" up a wall while filling in at its base. Planting one of these gives you two kinds of plant forms—mounding and climbing—for the price of one.

Potting benches and garden cupboards are getting to be so fashionable that they look good as a part of the garden. A small wooden shed used for tool storage can be an architectural part of the garden, and ready-to-assemble sheds come in styles to suit any design. If you don't want to keep your potting bench constantly tidy enough for visitors to see, or if you use one of those huge, molded plastic bins, then it's back to finding a way to disguise them.

Elegant Espalier for Walls and Fences

To espalier a plant means to train it to grow on a flat vertical surface. Turning a plant two-dimensional gives us more space in the small garden in which to move or to put more plants. Espaliered plants are usually grown against fences and walls, but sometimes, as woody plants mature and take on a more structural presence, they themselves become the fence. Those that are grown against a surface can be trained in several different designs, so that an apple tree can end up looking like a candelabrum or a fan. Some creative gardeners train their plants to look like windowpanes. Others choose a style called a Belgian fence. In this type of espalier, several plants are grown in a row, and their branches are trained at about 45-degree angles so that they crisscross, forming a pattern that is a series of diamond shapes.

A mature espaliered shrub or tree is part plant, part art. Not only does it fill up a blank wall, but it also can add elegance, whimsy, or formality to the garden.

Here are some tips for espaliering:

■ Many nurseries sell fruit trees especially grown for espalier; they already have that two-dimensional look to them. If you want a fruit tree espaliered, ask for these.

■ If you are choosing a shrub that has not been grown specifically for espalier, whether it be a witch hazel *(Hamamelis)* or a *Viburnum,* it's important to begin with a young plant that is suited to the form. Look for a plant with a few branches that are already growing in a flat fashion.

■ Choose the support on which you want to train the plant, and have it already installed before you plant. You can use a trellis or—for a dis-appearing support that will display more of the plant's form—a series of eyebolts and wires on a fence.

■ Freestanding supports of poles and wires for a woody plant such as an apple can be removed after several years, leaving a living fence.

■ Each year your pruning will consist of removing stems that don't conform to the pattern, while carefully bending and tying into form those stems that remain. It is easiest to bend new or one-year-old growth, but be careful when you start; some plants are more brittle than others. If you grow an apple as espalier, be sure not to trim off the short stems, known as spurs—those are where the flowers and fruit form.

■ Do not use wire directly on the stems, as this could cut through the bark and damage the plant. Instead, cover the wires at the points of contact, using a cushiony material (you can buy special tree guard material at the nursery, or you can use jute or even strips of old panty-hose). Eventually, not only will the plant develop a woody base (trunk), the stems that create the template will grow to be woody branches quite capable of remaining in the correct form without wires.

The Neighbor's Weeds

It's not as if you have so much room that you can give it away, yet often we find our small gardens, especially in the back, being encroached upon. That inevitable Northwest weed Himalayan blackberry creeps under or over the fence from your neighbor's weedy lot. Insidious bindweed slithers through cracks and winds its way around prized perennials before you know it's there. Huge tree limbs hang over, shading what you considered your only sunny patch and dropping leaves in your pond. Bamboo runs, and when it does, it seems to run right over to your place.

Cities deal with neighbor-against-neighbor complaints constantly. The first thing they ask you to do is try to work it out between the two of you. This can be exasperating if you have tried and it hasn't worked, or it can be intimidating because you haven't tried and really didn't want the confrontation. Still, you can avoid stress and worry by talking first.

If you've talked and it hasn't worked, yet you are reluctant to go to the city for mediation, try some exclusion techniques in your garden. Dig out any Himalayan blackberry or bamboo on your side of the fence, and then put in your own barrier. To exclude blackberries along the fence line, dig a trench about a foot deep and fill it with wood chips; every year you can rake them away and see what's trying to come through. Bamboo barriers need to be at least 24 inches deep to be effective; nurseries sell black plastic suited for this purpose. If a branch of a tree is overhanging your property, inform your neighbor that you will prune it for him—but do it properly, don't just whack off the limb. It wouldn't do you any good to end up looking at the stub of an ugly heading cut, and improper pruning promotes a mass of weak growth at the cut.

A common complaint is that a view is being blocked by a neighbor's tree. As tempted as you may be to take your chain saw to what you may consider a too-tall tree, it's better to talk about it. Relationships, as well as trees, have been ruined for views. Many municipalities have regulations regarding how high trees can be, what can be cut, and by whom. Call your city's parks and recreation, utilities, or neighborhood department to find out what you can and can't do. Especially, do not top trees (on your property or anyone else's); to do so is to invite disaster, and not just from the wrath of your neighbor. Topping weakens a tree and may well cause it to fall over in a storm.

Chapter Five

- ■ **Conditions in a Garden with No Ground**

- ■ **Pots, Containers, and Media**

- ■ **Plants for Balcony and Rooftop Gardens**

- ■ **Arranging the Balcony or Rooftop Garden**

- ■ **Caring for a Garden with No Ground**

Left: **Sheltered and shaded from the extreme heat of the day, this balcony hosts a luxurious garden, including *Hydrangea arborescens* 'Annabelle', Japanese forest grass (*Hakonechloa macra* 'Aureola'), and a hop vine.**

Balcony and Rooftop Gardens

The number of apartment- and condo-dwelling gardeners in the Northwest is on the rise. The fact that they have no ground doesn't deter them at all. Unwilling to give up gardening, or new to gardening but without a clue about where to start, people with balconies and rooftops look for likely corners for pots. Any available outdoor space is utilized: balconies get crowded with plants, and rooftops become jungles. Often, gardeners think that the only thing they can put out on a balcony are summer annuals—and even those get fried in the hot sun. It's frustrating to end up with dead or miserable-looking plants because of random plant selection, poor choice of containers, and erratic, overabundant, or nonexistent watering.

Space is at a premium on a balcony, and the climate is harsh there and on rooftops. But with planning and good choices you can create a lush garden that not only benefits you but does its small part toward greening our paved-over cities. With everything in pots of one kind or another, you must pay greater attention to water and sun, but you can grow much more than pansies and flowering kale in winter and petunias in summer. In reality, balcony and rooftop gardens can be as diverse and full of interest as any grounded garden. Trees, shrubs, vines, and roses can all be a part of the contained garden, sharing space with those pansies and petunias.

Experienced high-rise gardeners, though they be few, think nothing of hauling a few cubic yards of topsoil through the lobby, into the elevator of their building, and up to the tenth floor or the roof. Experience teaches them how big the sheet of plastic needs to be to cover the carpet, and how picking up stray bits they've dropped can do a lot for good will toward neighbors. Anything for the garden.

Conditions in a Garden with No Ground

Above: **This balcony has just enough space for a small table and a couple of chairs— and lots of plants. Crowding a sunny balcony with pots creates a lush garden feeling and helps cool things off.**

Most likely, the roof will not fall in if you have a garden on it. Weight and water are two concerns that come immediately to mind with a garden on a balcony or rooftop; yet those spaces hold furniture and accumulate rain, and we don't give that a second thought. Generally, pots and boxes pose no hazard, but if you feel the urge to create a garden that includes exceptionally heavy items, such as large landscape rocks or a planter box the length of the building, you may want to speak to the building engineer.

Of more concern to gardeners, of course, is the garden itself: the plants, which ones to choose, how they look, and how to take care of them. Conditions can be extreme on balconies and rooftops, and exposure plays a greater role than on the ground.

Climate and aspect affect how you garden on a balcony or rooftop. Apartment and condominium balconies in urban situations can be the victims of the "downtown canyon" effect. This is because wind sweeps down streets between tall buildings with much greater velocity (and drying capabilities) than through nearby neighborhoods of houses. Rooftops are windswept prairies, flat and open to the sky.

Rooftops will also most likely be in full sun, intensified by the reflected and radiated heat of the roof's surface. Balconies may get sun part of the day and then be plunged into darkness as the path of the

Below: **Although rooftops can accommodate most pots and plants, be sure to check with the building engineer first if you plan to install an extensive garden.**

sun goes behind your own or a nearby building. "Full sun" and "part shade" take on new meanings here. The sun is baking hot when it's there, and when it isn't, you have complete shade; there's nothing dappled about the sun's rays when they're blocked by a solid mass.

The Pacific Northwest benefits from many hours of sunlight during June, July, and August, and you can take advantage of this in your plant choices. Balconies that receive morning sun—at least four hours—may be able to grow plants that need full sun (even though "full sun" is normally considered to be at least six hours of direct sunlight). Use morning sunlight to your advantage by choosing plants that need half-day or full sun—but not those that prefer intense heat, such as the Mediterranean herbs rosemary and thyme, which would do better in the searing heat (reflected and radiated) of an afternoon-sun balcony.

You may want to create a shady oasis up on the hot roof. A wooden pergola—an arbor with a lattice roof—provides the support for vines that will create the shade for you. The classic choice is wisteria; its foot-long, fragrant blossom clusters are at their showy best as they hang through the holes in the lattice, tantalizing your nose. Vertical features such as pergolas, framed trellises, and container hedges also work on a design level. They break up the flatness of the roof, and they can help create a more dramatic view of a nearby building or distant mountain range by framing it.

Choose tough plants for exposed positions. Not only can they withstand the elements, they can be guardians for the rest of your garden. You can divert the wind with a rooftop hedge of bamboo or a broadleaf evergreen, such as golden elaeagnus (*Elaeagnus pungens* 'Maculata'); its leaves, with their broad yellow centers, will glow in the sun. Plants such as these provide protection for smaller plants that can't take drying winds.

Rooftops and balconies can accumulate enough rain so that you end up with wet feet and your pots don't drain well. Remedy this by building a boardwalk just a few inches off the surface (or, for a cheap fix, use wooden pallets). The spaces between the boards will let the water drain through, to the benefit of your feet and your potted plants.

Create a Rooftop Garden on Your Garage

If your garage has a flat roof, you might consider building a rooftop garden. You will need appropriate access, which means more than just a ladder pushed up against the side. A garage roof won't be as strong as the roof of a larger building, so don't go overboard with pots and planters until you know the roof's weight-bearing capacity. If you plan an extensive garden, have the roof checked by a structural engineer first. But after the safety is taken care of, you will have a high, sunny garden that can be lined with built-in containers or arranged with lightweight containers for herbs, vegetables, or flowers. It can be as much of an escape for you as any other secret garden.

Pots, Containers, and Media

Choosing Pots and Containers

Combine your artistic decorating tendencies with some practical reminders for selecting pots and containers:

■ Choose pots not only for how they look but also for what they will grow. Annuals and perennials can grow in pots just 6 inches deep (although you'll need to water several times a day in summer). Shrubs and trees need a minimum depth of 18 inches. The width of the pot depends on how many plants you want to squeeze in, but generally, woody plants need a width of 16 to 18 inches. Even so, you will need to repot every few years (see the section "Replanting Containers" later in this chapter).

■ Gardeners—like anyone else—can fall in love with the beautiful but impractical. Gorgeous, big, decorative glazed pots add an artistic note to the garden. Their shiny surfaces and deep blues and greens are luscious, but before you buy, look carefully at their shapes. Many come with an elegant contour that is narrow at the base, swelling in the middle, and narrowing again at the top. This isn't the container in which you want to plant trees, shrubs, or perennials (in other words, anything you might have to repot). The root ball will fill the available space (the wide part) and you won't be able to get it out of the narrow opening without sacrificing either the plant or the container.

■ Some containers, even unplanted, are so heavy that you won't ever want to move them around once they are in place. As long as they aren't too heavy for the building, that's fine, but how do you know when you'll want to adjust your garden? Six or eight inches one way or another may make a huge difference either to the arrangement or to your view. A heavy container can be on casters to make it easy to move around. This is not the most attractive look, so hide the casters by placing small pots around the base. Not only will this work for a disguise, you'll be creating a full, lush look with layers of plants.

■ If you have a black plastic nursery pot big enough for what you are planting, you can set it in a big basket (on an upturned empty pot if the basket is deep). Use a mulch of moss to hide the edges.

Below: **Plastic pots are lightweight and don't dry out as quickly as terra-cotta—qualities that obviously agree with this happy planting of summer pelargoniums.**

■ Choose a terra-cotta or concrete "look" in one of the newer containers that are actually made from a kind of foam resin. Their sides are typically decorated with garlands and cherubs, reminiscent of Italian designs. Classical shapes, such as the white Versailles-style planter boxes, now are made in lightweight plastic.

■ If you long for the been-there-for-ages look without the weight of concrete or metal, create a faux-antique. Take a plastic container in a classic shape—an urn, for example—and treat it with a two-step process. First apply "Instant Iron," then spray it with a product called "Instant-Rust." In a few days, your container will look as though it's been outdoors for a century or two. Ask at your hardware store or search the Internet for these two bizarre but amazing products.

Choosing the Media

Managing containerized plants is easier when you use a good-quality planting medium to which you have added extra organic matter. Many of the soil mixes available work well in containers.

When buying a bag of potting "soil," read the bag and you'll see that what you've got isn't really soil. Soil is made up of minerals, and it is formed when wind and water slough off bits of rock. The collection of minerals, along with about 5 percent organic matter, makes up what we call "soil" in the garden. The bag of potting mix is made up of shredded bark, perlite (a puffy, white, volcanic rock that lightens the mix), compost, and sometimes vermiculite (another volcanic rock that looks like shiny flakes of mica); these ingredients come in varying percentages, depending on the brand.

This kind of mixture is well suited for container culture. It's light, absorbs water, and has a small amount of nutrient value. Also, it is sterile, which means you're not bringing disease pathogens into the pot. Adding one-quarter to one-third compost by volume to it enriches the mix and helps keep it well-draining.

Plants for Balcony and Rooftop Gardens

Your choice of plants for the potted garden is driven by size and exposure. But there are ways you can get around even those constraints.

Small gardens often force gardeners to choose small plants. Your eyes are always drawn to cultivar names such as 'Nana' or 'Compacta', thinking that those will be small enough to stay in your potted garden. You would love to have a Persian ironwood tree (*Parrotia persica*), with its fabulous flaming fall color, but you know that after five or six years, it will be too big—and that'll be way before it reaches its mature 30-foot spread. It's time to take advantage of the garden network. Mature plants (or those on their way to maturity) are valuable—just go and price a big tree at a nursery. When your young tree gets too big for its balcony, you could donate it to a school, public garden, or demonstration garden and, with an arborist's assessment of its value, get a tax deduction. Maybe you know a gardener who will pay you for it, or someone with whom you can exchange for something in kind (housecleaning? weeding? painting?). You will get several years of enjoyment from one plant, and you'll get to buy a new plant when the too-large one has found a new home.

Apart from size considerations, study the extreme conditions of your garden. Plants in containers are more at risk than plants in the garden and more dependent on you for their needs, so there's no point in putting them under more stress with inappropriate sun or shade placement.

If your rooftop has unrelenting sunshine (and balconies may suffer the same), things can heat up quickly and stay hot. Provide relief for yourself (and several containers) by building a wide, square trellis for robust vines that will offer shade from the heat. Think of fragrant wisteria blossoms dangling down to brush your head as you pass, or maybe even a cluster of grapes. Both of these vines provide lush foliage (the big leaves of a grapevine are especially dramatic) that creates an oasis underneath. Deciduous plants that are used as a heat screen in summer will, in winter, let in what sunshine there is to help warm the indoors.

Mixing and matching woody plants with perennials and annuals gives the potted garden a full look, but because different plants may have different water or fertilizer needs, it's often easier to keep each type of plant in its own pot. That way, you can provide the regular fertilizer that annuals need, and you can also rearrange the pots, keeping a fresh look and seasonal look to the garden.

Below: **It's small now, but the grape vine growing in a pot has the potential to reach 30 feet and may eventually need a more permanent spot.**

Annuals in Pots

Known for their long season of bloom, annuals are fun, fast, and floriferous. They make perfect container candidates, and in the mild climate of the Pacific Northwest they will put on a show from March to November. In the garden, this means digging or pulling up annuals at the end of their season, and this can damage the root systems of neighboring perennials and leave unsightly holes in the garden plan.

In containers, the water and nutrient needs of annuals are easier to meet. In addition to the fertilizer you incorporated into the planting mix, annuals should be fertilized every two to three weeks during spring and through the summer. Timed-release fertilizer works well here, as does a weak solution of fish fertilizer in the watering can. All annuals need extra nutrients because they bloom almost continuously; but in addition annuals in pots have no access to the nutrients present in garden soil.

The usual list of annuals—pansies, fuchsias, and begonias for shade; petunias, verbenas, and sunflowers for sun—needn't be considered common and boring. Why argue with success? These annuals are popular precisely because they bloom well, come in a huge variety of colors and forms, and can be mixed and matched for new looks. Use these tried-and-true plants; but look for different colors and forms than the ones you've used before.

■ Instead of pansies with huge, heavy flowers (so heavy, in fact, that they hang their heads and you never get to admire their pretty faces), choose the smaller flowers of the pure orange 'Padparadja' or the chocolate- and glowing-bronze flowers of 'Irish Molly'.

■ Petunia strains, too, were selected to be big and blowsy, and it's gotten so that a light rain can collapse their huge flowers. Now, smaller-flowered petunias are available. Some of the most popular selections are from the Surfina strain (pink, purple, and magenta), which grow as trailing plants. These have been hybridized from the species *Petunia integrifolia*. A plant that looks like a petunia and has even smaller flowers is *Calibrachoa*. These plants, labeled as "Million Bells" at nurseries, come in pink, blue, red, purple, and a lovely apricot called 'Terra Cotta'.

Above: **High summer may be a glorious time for annuals such as this char-treuse pelargonium and dark-leaved nasturtium, but they also will continue to flourish until frost.**

■ Just because it's in a pot doesn't mean it has to be short. Well-anchored pots can hold tall annuals, and the sight of a 3-foot *Cleome* (spider flower) topped with its whiskery flowers, swaying in the breeze, adds not only height but movement to your potted garden.

■ Grow sunflowers; if you don't want the 8-foot variety, look for the mix 'Music Box', a cultivar that tops out at about 3 feet.

■ Many plants have such interesting foliage that they can set off the flower show or be the show themselves. Love-lies-bleeding *(Amaranthus)* has bizarre, pendulous red flowers, but also comes in selections, such as 'Illumination', where the variegated leaves are red, pink, yellow, and gold. Licorice plant *(Helichrysum petiolare)* is a trailer with silver-gray leaves; it is also available variegated and in a yellow-green form ('Limelight'). And there are dozens and dozens of *Coleus* cultivars; foliage colors range from maroon and gold to lime, red, and pink. You can tone down the wild colors and patterns by pairing them with plants with solid green leaves.

If you are unsure what annuals to try, your local nursery is poised to help. In early spring, browse the aisles, look at the display pots, talk to nursery workers and other customers; you'll soon have a trunkful of plants to bring home.

In mild Northwest winters, many plants that we consider annuals (pansies, snapdragons, and pelargoniums, for example) can live over until the next spring. If that happens, take advantage of another year of flowers by cutting back the old foliage and repotting (see "Replanting Containers" later in this chapter).

Perennials in Containers

Pots of annuals can keep a garden in flower for months and months, while perennials add seasonal interest. The year-round look of trees and shrubs gives a balcony or rooftop garden an established feeling.

When you plant a container, don't add Styrofoam worms or other fill material in the bottom to make it lighter unless you're planting annuals that don't need much soil. All you are doing is decreasing root space (and adding to your own work, because you'll have to water more frequently). In temporary plantings of annuals, and even perennial combinations that you intend to undo when the season is over, soil volume may not be a concern; more permanently planted containers, however, need the soil space. Trees and shrubs need about 18 inches of soil, so it isn't worth it to fill in the bottom 6 inches of space in a 2-foot-high pot.

Always add more organic matter to the potting medium before you plant. Well-composted manure or yard waste lightens the mixture and adds some nutrients, particularly micronutrients, that may be missing in the manufactured potting soil.

Below: **In this sprightly container, sky-blue lobelia combines with flashy foliage, including a variegated euonymus and licorice plant (*Helichrysum petiolare* 'Limelight').**

Be wary of so-called water-holding material. Polymers are added to container potting media to provide water when the soil dries out. Dry pellets or chunks of material soak up water to many times their size and hold it until the surrounding soil is dry, at which time they begin to release the moisture. In theory, polymers decrease the need for watering and save your plants before they are stressed out, but actual research has shown mixed results. If you decide to use polymers, don't forget to check both the soil moisture and the overall look of your plants on a regular basis. It's easy to spot a wilted plant, but even before a plant wilts from lack of water you may see some signs—for example, the leaves may turn dark, with a purplish cast.

Unless you're growing a bog garden in a pot, a drainage hole is a must. Don't be tempted to cover the drainage hole with a piece of crockery to keep the soil in—the soil isn't going anywhere, although you may see a little of it drain out during the first few waterings. You can place trays or pans under pots to keep water from running off, but if your balcony garden is open to rain, you'll need to watch that standing water doesn't form in the trays.

Fertilize perennials and woody shrubs in containers yearly. Container plants don't have the benefit of normal soil activity to provide nutrients. Fertilize woody shrubs by scratching in a dry 5-5-5 fertilizer at half the recommended amount. Perennials that stay in containers also need a yearly dose of fertilizer.

Below: **A balcony full of pots needs attention with fertilizer and water. Don't assume that using water-holding materials such as polymers can substitute for checking the dryness of the soil yourself.**

Bamboo in Containers

Gardeners who fear bamboo and its aggressive ways can experiment with it in containers. Bamboo adds life to a garden. A breeze sets it swaying, and its rustling, waterlike sound is a good mask for traffic noise. Although bamboos are divided roughly into runners and clumpers, even the clumpers will go places eventually. This is why bamboo is not a plant for the open garden unless you take precautions (the best defense, remember, is a good offense). In a container, clumping varieties can stay for five or six years before they need to be repotted, but even the running type will live happily contained for about three years.

Bamboo doesn't like to dry out, so most selections prefer to be sited out of the way of drying winds. Drying winds may be the very definition of your balcony or rooftop, but you might be able to find a corner for a pot, or use a long planter against a wall that gets part shade.

Bamboo is a member of the grass family, and as such has its growing points (where we see leaves unfurl on other plants) below ground. What we call bamboo "stems" are really culms. Running bamboo sends underground structures called rhizomes far and wide, and new culms grow off those, up through the soil (and into the neighbor's garden). Clumping bamboo has rhizomes that are short and thick, sending culms up over a more compact area.

Choose pots for bamboo that are no more than 2 inches wider than the container in which they come. These include black bamboo *(Phyllostachys nigra),* with culms that grow 4 to 10 feet and turn ebony in the sun; fountain bamboo *(Fargesia nitida),* which grows to 15 feet, has purple culms, and will grow in shade; and the small *Sasa veitchii,* which grows to 4 feet tall and has leaves that are edged in creamy white in winter.

More bamboos that will withstand a pot for up to six years

before needing to be divided include *Fargesia murieliae,* which grows to 9 feet and has arching stems; white-stripe bamboo *(Pleioblastus argenteostriatus),* which grows to 3 feet and has white or yellow stripes on its blue-green leaves; and yellow-stripe bamboo *(P. viridistriatus),* which grows to 3 feet. When considering the height of your bamboo, remember that, set up in containers, these lower-growing bamboos will really look 2 or 3 feet taller.

Arranging the Balcony or Rooftop Garden

Arranging the Pots

Because annuals can live happily in containers as shallow as 6 inches, your arrangements can be changing constantly. Small pots make the garden easy to move around (although small containers dry out in an instant, so you'll need to be ready with water). With many small pots, you can arrange and rearrange to your heart's content.

■ Line up pots of pelargoniums along the balcony railing. For more security, attach a bracket for each pot or use wire pot hanger racks.

■ Cluster small pots of annuals around larger containers. Vary the heights—adding interest as well as allowing the whole picture to be seen at once—by setting some of the pots on top of upturned empty pots.

■ Set pots on step stools and boxes, and then hide these homely props behind other pots and foliage. You don't have to spend a fortune on different-sized pots when many of them won't even be seen. Be creative with the façade, and put your money into the plants.

Arranging the Balcony Garden

Your balcony may be just big enough for a few pots around the perimeter and a corner grouping. Use several pots to make the space feel lush, and disguise the limits of the garden.

Select a plant that is tall and slender for the back, perhaps a columnar selection of the evergreen shrub Japanese holly *(Ilex crenata),* such as 'Sky Sentry' (also known as 'Sky Pencil'). This is also a good plant to use in a line along the perimeter, as a scrim more than a screen. Make the plant in the back taller by putting its pot on top of another upturned pot or a small stool.

In front of the corner plant, arrange variously sized pots with more rounded forms. On a full-sun balcony, you can use this as your herb garden, with sage, thymes, and a small rosemary such as 'Blue Boy' or a lavender (small 'Blue Cushion' or jumbo 'Giant Hidcote').

Many plant choices are available for the shadier balcony, too. The aforementioned Japanese holly takes shade. A shady balcony would accommodate pots of almost-evergreen foamflower *(Tiarella)*; the cultivars 'Skeleton Key' and 'Iron Butterfly' have interesting dark variegation on their leaves. Or try the closely related coral bells *(Heuchera)*, which has cultivars with dark purple leaves ('Stormy Seas') and grayish leaves ('Pewter Veil'). Hostas, also good for shade, come in a huge range of variegation and grow well in containers.

Below: **A collection of pots adds interest with varying heights and plant forms, such as hens and chicks *(Sempervivum)* in the duck planter, gray *Sedum*, and the large rosette of *Echeveria*.**

Arranging the Rooftop Garden

Create your own walls on the rooftop. Rooftops often don't have the backdrop of a wall or railing, but they do have open skies and city skylines. These make dramatic settings, but they don't provide any definition to the garden, so a line of potted evergreens can become the wall needed to set off the colors of flowers and shrubs. Often this hedge will also serve as a windbreak, keeping other plants from drying out. A great expanse of flatness can be unnerving for some people; a hedge on the roof will keep you from feeling as though you're flying away.

Arrange the garden for the winter view

from indoors. You may not spend much time in winter sitting out in your balcony or rooftop garden, but you can probably see it from indoors every day. At the end of summer or late in the fall, depending on when your gardening season ends, rearrange the pots so that your garden makes a pleasing display from the kitchen table or living room sofa—wherever you spend those dark days planning next year's garden.

This is where broadleaf and coniferous evergreens come in handy. Their presence in winter gives life to even the tiny balcony garden—so much better than looking at the bare concrete! The play of the cream-edged leaves of *Pieris* 'Variegata' (with the added bonus of flowers that develop over winter) against the darker sprays of a Hinoki cypress *(Chamaecyparis obtusa)* 'Nana Gracilis' is a good effect. And many dwarf conifers take on bronze or coppery tones in winter. For late fall and winter flowers, you can use the evergreen *Camellia sasanqua*. These are often Lax shrubs, and look best in containers when they have some trellis support, but some, such as 'Yuletide', with

Below: **A wall of plants, including a low arborvitae hedge, acts as a windbreak while disguising the dropoff.**

single, dark red blooms, are more compact. Early bulbs—including crocus, *Iris reticulata,* snowdrops, and early small daffodils such as 'Tete-a-Tete'—will also give you a colorful show in winter.

Caring for a Garden with No Ground

Watering

If you have a small balcony, it won't be too difficult to take the watering can (or teakettle) out to the pots. Larger balconies and rooftops may have water spigots, and there a short or coiled hose may make more sense. Coiled hoses—even though they may stretch up to 50 feet—retract into a compact form; but, just like phone cords, they do have a tendency to become twisted. Emitter watering systems consist of thin, black coiled hoses that can be woven through and around the contained garden; at each pot, an emitter is placed that sprays or drips water. Emitter systems can be run manually or on a timer.

Watering is a tricky affair in the container garden. During the summer, and especially if your balcony or rooftop is windy, the rate at which plants lose moisture is greatly accelerated. Water is drawn up from the roots and lost through the leaves in mere hours, and this isn't occurring only in the sun—it happens in dry, windy shade too. Container potting mixes watered in the morning can become bone dry by afternoon. Once this kind of mix is dry, you'll have a devil of a time rewetting it, although a few drops of dishwashing liquid on the surface of the pot will help.

Rooftops and uncovered balcony gardens get the full brunt of wet Northwest winters. If your balcony or rooftop garden is usually waterlogged in winter, protect your plants from drowning by keeping the pots up off the flat surface. Use "pot feet," which you can find in styles from utilitarian (casters or rollers that are mostly hidden from view) to whimsical (duck feet or human toes). Besides helping with drainage, this will also keep clay pots from absorbing much of the excess water, which will in turn lessen the possibility of the pots freezing and cracking.

Overwintering

Plant winter annuals to take the place of summer flowers. Pull out summer annuals in late October or early November—after all, they aren't supposed to last more than one growing season. Winter annuals, planted up in October, can act as placeholders until spring. Flowering kale will look good until about February, after which it grows too tall, with leafless stems. Pansies will last into March and April, and by then you're ready for something new.

The least hardy part of a plant is its root system, and roots in containers are particularly vulnerable to cold weather. In the ground, roots are well protected from occasional freezing temperatures, so we are usually more concerned about stems and buds. But in pots, roots may have only an inch of protection between them and freezing air. If the weather report calls for sustained below-freezing weather in your area, take heed. Protect those roots by wrapping your containers in layers of burlap or old sheets. If you have several small pots, treating them as a unit may be more successful. Gather pots together, fill up the spaces and around the edges with wadded-up newspapers, and then wrap or secure with plastic or cloth. Don't tie plastic around a trunk and leave it, though, because the subsequent condensation (as the temperatures warm up) would be a breeding environment for disease.

The hardiness of stems, leaves, and flowers depends on the plant. Winter-blooming plants such as witch hazel *(Hamamelis)* adapt to the cold by closing up their flowers in freezing weather. Early bulbs such as crocus, *Iris reticulata,* and snowdrops *(Galanthus)* come out of snow and cold air unscathed, as do the shoots of daffodils and tulips that peek out early. But bring the pots of florist's cyclamen indoors when cold weather hits.

Replanting Containers

Permanently planted containers need to be revitalized. Any container medium will pack down over time, and perennials, shrubs, and trees may grow out of the pots in which they started. Plants suited to container culture can go for many years without being taken out. But when water seems to run right through a container, that's a sign that the pot holds mostly roots and little soil. It's time to repot.

■ Spread out a tarp to catch the mess.

■ With a trowel or a short-handled shovel, dig out each plant and place it on the tarp. (This is sometimes easier said than done, especially if there is more than one plant in a container.) If the plants seem to be one solid mass, use a garden fork (short-handled, with tines like a pitchfork, but sturdier). Plunge the tines into the root mass and rock it back and forth to loosen the root balls from each other. You may want to lay the pot on its side and work the plants out that way.

Below: **Small pots are more likely to expose root systems to freezing temperatures, so be sure to move these susceptible containers to a protected spot for the winter.**

■ Protect the exposed root balls by covering them with a damp towel or burlap while you're working.

■ Dig out several inches' worth of potting medium (up to half) from the container, add back compost and fresh potting medium, and mix well.

■ Potbound plants need to have their roots loosened, and woody plants may need to be root-pruned. Roots that are growing in a circle can be teased out with a hand cultivator (the tool with three prongs). It won't hurt to cut off the last few inches of these roots, as they aren't doing the plant any good (this is known as root-pruning). If a plant is severely potbound, the roots will be brown or yellow (live roots are usually white). Check to see that there are no kinks in the way the roots are growing. Kinked roots don't straighten themselves out, and when left on trees and shrubs these kinks continue to thicken, eventually cutting off the plant's supply of water and nutrients.

■ If the medium is dry, dampen the mix before putting the plants back. Don't fill the pot up to the brim with mix; leaving an inch of space will keep the water from spilling over the edge. Water well.

Left: **Plants, paving, and a place to sit all vie for space in the small patio garden. Here, the gardener has achieved a balance by creating a circle in a square, giving the plants more room at the corners.**

Courtyard, Patio, and Deck Gardens

The back garden is part of our living space in these modern times, and in the Northwest we eagerly await good weather to begin the season of outdoor living. Often our back garden is an extension of our house: French doors open onto an area we treat as a combination kitchen (the barbecue), den (a quiet chair in which to sit and read), and entertainment center (birds at the feeder). Blurring the lines between inside and out can help both the garden and the indoors seem roomier.

A patio, courtyard, or deck can be a lifeless place without plants, and plants (unless you go for fake greenery) mean maintenance. But striking a balance between paved area and plants—and sometimes just finding a place to put a plant plus a table and chairs—isn't always easy. There's no way around maintenance, but thoughtful plant selection and placement will lessen any problems you may encounter.

The hard surfaces of courtyards, patios, and decks can help to erase the boundary between garden and house by providing a little of both. This is valuable in small spaces, as both the outside and inside will seem bigger when those lines are blurred. You can also move some furniture outdoors and some plants indoors. Houses and apartments with French or sliding doors, or extensive windows, help make the garden seem part of an indoor room. And looking out onto a table and chairs, set in the summer with a floral tablecloth and a pot of nasturtiums, makes you think your dining room has doubled in size.

The intimate space of courtyard, patio, or deck may be the very place for which you head when you get home from work. When you are selecting plants, think about what time of day you most enjoy sitting in the garden. Four-o'clocks, Grecian windflowers *(Anemone blanda)*, and anything else that opens during the day and closes as the light fades may not be the best choices, since their show will be over before your time in the garden has begun.

Patios aren't limited to the back of the house. Build a patio in the front garden if your view is better, or if you enjoy the neighborhood and long for more of a community feel. In the summer, you'll draw neighbors like bees to sit down with a glass of iced tea. Front-garden patios, like front stoops, are for watching the world go by. But on a patio, you can barbecue while you're watching.

The Small Courtyard Garden

A courtyard is a small garden that is surrounded by walls on at least three sides. Courtyards are becoming more popular in Northwest cities as condominium and townhouse complexes are built; courtyards are designed to add a bit of privacy to close-quarters living. Since they are on ground level, they help greatly with moderating the temperature because the soil, even under paving, is slow to heat and cool. Courtyards are also more "grounded," because you have ground-level views; for example, you look up to see trees. The view over the railing of a balcony or off the side of a rooftop will immediately tell you that you are suspended, but in a courtyard what you see around you is on terra firma.

The history of courtyard gardens is tied to their provenance. The ornamental gardens of Italy, Spain, and other countries around the Mediterranean region were places to escape the heat. Often set in the middle of the house, with all doors opening onto it, the courtyard offered relief by being shady (at least for part of the day) yet open to fresh air. The spray of water from a fountain was refreshing, and even the sound of the water had a cooling effect. Plants transpired, and the humidity they created in these arid climates also helped to make the air feel cooler (air traveling through water to cool things off is the basis for the evaporative cooling systems known as "swamp coolers").

In the Northwest, we usually want to do just the opposite. The colors and styles of materials and plants in our courtyards can add a few degrees to the temperature just by implication. Use the idea of a Mediterranean courtyard with warm colors of flowers, yellow-variegated foliage, and floor selections in terra-cotta colors, and our cool Northwest climate can feel a few degrees warmer. It's an illusion, the same as the sound of water from a fountain helping to cool us off.

Here are some other tips for making the most of your courtyard garden:

■ **Take advantage of the courtyard's extra warmth.** Courtyards capture what heat there is, and reflect and radiate it. Because they are entirely paved, courtyards are particularly good at this. The sun that hits the garden, often from about midday to midafternoon, can add quite a few degrees. (A true Mediterranean garden would have a huge shade tree at the side of the house to help reduce heat.) Use the added warmth for a longer outdoor season for houseplants, which often spend the summer outside.

■ **Select the right trees.** Space is at a premium when the sides of your garden are walls. You can't plant a tree whose canopy will spread over into the neighbor's garden. Choose small trees for new plantings, and enjoy them for many years. For that essential Mediterranean look, grow a bay tree in a terra-cotta pot in the center of a sunny courtyard. Although they're hardy to USDA Zone 7, bays can be damaged by severe Northwest winters; in a courtyard, the tree will be more protected.

■ **Use a water feature.** Classic courtyard design usually includes a large fountain right smack in the middle, which takes up a great deal of room. If all you're going to do is walk through the courtyard or look out onto it, this may be fine, but if you want to sit in the garden, the fountain will have to move aside. A smaller water feature can be accommodated in a corner, leaving room for a table and chairs. Wall fountains take up almost no room, give you a water sound, and are available in classic or modern designs. (See "Can I Have a Water Feature?" in Chapter Seven.)

■ **Optimize space for garden entertaining.** Square tables take up less room than round ones (there's always a straight side to scoot around), even though you may not be able to squeeze as many chairs around them. If you have space indoors, choose a small table and a few chairs that can work inside as well as outside. Remember to leave enough room around pots to walk comfortably. Don't plant prickly shrubs, such as roses and barberry, where you'll be likely to brush up against them.

■ **Create a piece of art.** Looking out on the courtyard garden is like looking at a painting. It's framed, it's got glass in front of it—it must be art. If you spend more time looking at your courtyard garden from inside than you actually spend in it, arrange it for that purpose. Organize vignettes of pots so they can be admired from the most obvious viewpoints. In a shady spot, place a collection of pots to make a complete picture: one with a tall, slender evergreen, one mound of dwarf azalea or rhododendron, and one seasonal display of bright, spiky, and trailing annuals.

Feature your favorite art in this "gallery." Such a defined and solid space shows off artwork well, almost better than when it gets engulfed by foliage in the open garden. The fountain, whether it be a central feature or a wall fountain, is a perfect example: it can lend an ancient Roman or a Moorish look that's particularly appropriate in a courtyard. Stone planters (the devil to move around, but fabulous when in place) and stone plaques are much more "on display" in the courtyard than in other garden settings.

Trees in Courtyards and Patios

A tree in the middle of a paved area is a focal point that draws the eye. The form you choose can even suggest a style: an upright form implies formality and stiffness, while a spreading shape, especially one broader than it is tall, gives the impression of comfort. Broadly spreading trees create the best shade. Even a small tree (to 20 or 25 feet high, with the same spread) can offer enough relief from the summer sun that you can set a small table and chairs underneath. A deciduous tree in this case would make an effective scrim between you and the sun, the traffic, or a nearby high-rise.

If you are building a patio and want to keep an existing tree, consider its needs:

■ If a tree is placed where you want to build a patio or courtyard, you can work around it, because excavation to build these surfaces doesn't go down many inches.

■ Even better, you may want to build up the courtyard just a few inches so that the large, woody anchor roots of the tree are left intact. Trees can take a fair amount of damage to their root system; trees transplanted from one place to another often begin a new life with only 25 percent of their root system. With special care for a couple of years, they are fine. But the anchor roots of an existing tree are part of what keeps the tree upright, and so it's unwise to go cutting through them, assuming that they will regenerate in a short time.

Below: **In this fountain, water drips down walls behind a terra-cotta figure, on its way to draining below.**

■ Leave at least 3 feet in diameter unpaved around the tree. This will accommodate trunk growth, because a trunk is usually flared (wider at the base than higher up).

■ Do not mortar the paving around an existing tree, because you are then cutting off much of the water supply to the roots. The 3-foot-diameter space that you leave around the trunk isn't where the slender, hairlike feeder roots are—they have grown far and wide, even wider than the tree's canopy. If the bricks or pavers of the patio are held in place by a rigid frame, you can sift sand between them for a solid surface. This will keep the water channel open to the tree's roots.

Debating whether to plant a tree in a courtyard or patio? Many gardeners want the shade and the soft look that a tree brings to a large paved area but don't want the chore of cleaning up fallen leaves, flowers, and fruit. Some trees are less messy than others, but unless you opt for a plastic tree, you will have to rake. (Worried about leaves staining the concrete? Think of it as art—people pay more money for decorated pavers than plain ones.) Avoid trees with large, soft fruit; instead, go for a Japanese maple or a flowering, not fruiting, cherry. (See the "Trees" list at the back of this book.)

Patio Surfaces

A patio may be surrounded on two sides by walls or it may be open, with only the house as definition. Its floor may be poured concrete, or it may be made of bricks or stone. Containers decorate the flat surface and give a sense of privacy.

As with a courtyard, the solid surface of a patio can add warmth as it reflects, absorbs, and radiates heat from the sun. Unless there are trees shading portions of it, the patio may be the warmest garden area you have; take advantage of this by selecting plants that need warmth, such as peaches or figs.

Choose the patio material to suit your style:

■ Flagstones, laid in a crazy-quilt pattern, set an informal tone (although too much craziness is hard on the eyes).

To Mortar or Not to Mortar

Below: **An unmortared patio allows rainfall and water from the hose to soak into the ground instead of running off to the city's storm-water drainage.**

We are paving over the world in rapid fashion, and many of our small gardens are already surrounded by the solid, impenetrable surfaces—walls, sidewalks, streets, parking lots. It will help not only our gardens, which need the rain (even in the Northwest we have water shortages), but also our beleaguered storm drain systems if we allow as much rain as possible to permeate the soil naturally instead of being whisked off to the gutter. When they are mortared together, bricks, pavers, or flagstones create a solid surface that does not allow rainwater to seep into the soil. But the same patio materials, if set closely together without mortar, framed with edging so that they won't shift, can have the small cracks between them filled with sand. Sand allows water to drain through—and it even allows you to grow small plants that enjoy the heat of the moment. If you find weeds coming up in the cracks, try a low-key approach to control: pour boiling water on them, or spray full-strength kitchen-grade vinegar. When the foliage withers, it's easy to pull up the offenders.

■ Bricks are cut to form a consistent size, and can be laid straight or in patterns that include herringbone, basket weave, and even—a test for the mathematician in you—circular. Patterns are always more apparent in patios than on paths because patios are larger.

■ Other cut materials include the concrete pavers that mimic cobble-stone. For something other than gray, concrete can be dyed to tints of brick, blue, or green. Interlocking cut concrete pieces form their own pattern as you lay them.

■ Under gray Northwest winter skies, gray stone may look too cold to you. In that case, choose material with a warm tone. A patio floor with an orange-pink cast goes particularly well with terra-cotta pots.

Crushed-Rock Surfaces

Any patio will need to be framed by, for example, an edging of bricks or rigid, brown plastic strips that become almost invisible. With such a frame, you will be able to use some form of crushed rock for a patio. Quarter-minus, the unsifted rock that includes rock dust, packs down on top of sand to make a smooth, solid, even surface that will take weather, furniture, and foot traffic in stride. It gives a unified look to the patio, stays put well, and is particularly valuable in small spaces where pouring concrete might be difficult. And, if necessary, it can be removed more easily than mortared pavers. Raking fallen leaves off it is easy, and you'll never have to worry about a slick surface on a frosty morning. Even throughout soggy Northwest winters, when bare ground squishes to the footfall, crushed rock drains well and provides a solid surface.

Crushed rock comes in many forms and sizes. The name always indicates the size, and if it also includes smaller sizes of particles all the way to dust, the name will include "minus." Quarter-minus consists of pieces from a quarter inch in diameter all the way to dust (it's also called "number 4 to dust" or specifically said to contain "fines"); 5/8-inch minus and 3/4-inch minus are also available. If the material has been sifted so that it does not include smaller pieces or dust, it will be called only by the size: quarter-inch, five-eighths-inch, and so on.

The particles that make up crushed rock have edges, in contrast to gravel, which is rounded. A surface of crushed rock can have just as neat and formal an appearance as a solid surface, and this material is a particularly good choice where drainage is poor. A word of caution: If the underlying soil doesn't drain well, then the patio (or path) won't either. If the soil where you want to put in a patio is mucky, it's a good idea to put in a drainage system first, and then use sifted rather than unsifted crushed rock; the uniformly larger pieces will allow water to drain through more readily.

Provided it's laid on a bed of sand, a patio of any material should remain fairly level. This is more important with large areas such as a patio, because teetering tables and chairs are not ideal for entertaining. (A path can often get away with being more rustic.) To keep the patio as level as possible:

■ You'll need to dig down 6 to 8 inches and place edging or a frame of wood or plastic to hold materials in.

■ Plastic edging is available at most large home and garden stores, and can be cut to fit.

■ In the dug-out area, place a 2- or 3-inch layer of crushed rock or other material with edges (not round gravel), packed down.

■ Put a 1-inch layer of builder's sand on top (also packed down). You may be able to use a roller to compact and level these materials. (A roller looks like a large, smooth barrel with a push-handle. Fill it with water to make it heavy.)

■ If you don't have room to run a roller through, a 2-by-4 cut to fit the width of the path can take its place. Use it to tamp the materials down.

■ After that, you can place the pavers of your choice.

Bulbs That Brighten

When we hear the word "bulb" we usually picture the ubiquitous riot of color in spring that begins with crocuses, progresses through daffodils, and ends with tulips. What we often forget is that it's possible to have bulbs blooming in the garden at all times of the year—from autumn *Colchicum* to summer ornamental onions. Fall- and winter-flowering bulbs are particularly welcome in the Northwest, when the perennials are gone and the world is dark.

Incorporating bulbs into the small garden often means choosing plants with smaller flowers—and smaller leaves. Emperor and Darwin tulips may dazzle in spring, but their long, wide leaves—which you must not cut off, because they are providing food for the bulb—die a slow and ugly death. If you can't do without jumbo tulips and daffodils, you can treat them as annuals, digging them up after the spring show. Or you can confine them to pots, planted up in fall, covered with a layer of cheerful winter pansies or small evergreen tufts of an ornamental grass such as *Festuca glauca* 'Elijah Blue' or the tufted hair grass *Deschampsia caespitosa*. The bulbs emerge, the flowers amaze, and then you can replant the pots or move them to a less conspicuous spot while the leaves turn yellow and wither.

Save the small garden—and especially such close-up sections of courtyards, patios, and decks—for more permanently planted pots, and include some of the wide range of smaller bulbs available. Their dying leaves can be disguised by the emerging foliage of plants such as hostas.

Beginning in fall, a mass of hardy *Cyclamen hederifolium* can carpet the ground under shrubs and trees with its shades of pink; in winter, *C. coum* takes over. Both species are small (4 to 6 inches high) and have heart-shaped leaves, often mottled with silver, that die back by summer; both species grow well in shade. Snowdrops (*Galanthus* spp.), which grow 6 to 8 inches high, have white flowers (sometimes edged in green). Many gardeners have more success planting snowdrops "in the green," instead of dormant bulbs.

Below: **The tender bulb** *Gladiolus callianthus* (often listed as *Acidanthera bicolor* or *A. murieliae*) **opens its graceful white, highly fragrant flowers in late summer.**

It's easy to tuck the corms of crocuses into corners and along walks around the garden. When their late-winter flowers fade, the grassy foliage remains as tufts and then neatly fades away. Other bulbs for late winter and early spring include the small narcissi such as *Narcissus* 'Tete-a-Tete' and *N. bulbocodium*, the latter known for its yellow flowers that look like tiny hoop petticoats. *Chionodoxa*, which grows to about 6 inches and has blue, star-shaped flowers, is another small bulb that rewards close-up viewing. Windflower *(Anemone blanda)* opens its daisylike white, blue, or pink flowers to the sun, and closes at night; its cutleaf foliage dies back soon after the flowers fade.

There are tulips that fit well into the small garden both because of their smaller stature and because they return to bloom year after year—unlike some of the larger hybrids, which dwindle down to a few puny flowers after three or four years. The cultivars of *Tulipa kaufmanniana* are known as water-lily tulips; they grow about 8 inches high, and when the flowers open wide on sunny days, they reveal two-toned colors. *Greigii* tulips are also reliable bloomers year after year. They grow up to 14 inches high and bloom in early to mid spring.

In summer, ornamental onions create balls of color with their clusters of flowers. From the 12-inch-high *Allium moly* 'Jeannine' with its sunny yellow flowers to the soccer ball–sized purple flowers of *A. cristophii* or the fireworks heads of *A. schubertii* (even the seed heads are attractive), you can find an onion to fit. For tall, slender elegance, use the onion relative *Nectaroscordum siculum*; it grows about 3 feet high, and has upright buds that open to dangling pink-and-green-striped flowers.

Use perennials to hide fading bulb foliage. The leaves of *Heuchera*, *Tiarella*, and wild ginger *(Asarum)* can be used as high ground covers (at about 6 to 8 inches) that let the leaves of small *Narcissus* and other bulbs drop below.

The Patio Border

If you pave the patio all the way to the fence, it prevents you from having an in-the-ground garden. So, if possible, create a garden by leaving a 3-foot border of soil between the edge of the patio and the fence. Maintenance will be easy in this small border: 3 feet is just about as far as you can reach when you're weeding. It won't be much to water; you can hand-water, lay soaker hoses, or install a drip system. A border around the patio is an easy way to deal with limited space in the small garden, because you don't have to make decisions about its shape and style. And plants along the fence visually soften the hard planes of both fence and patio.

Creating a raised bed is one attractive option for this border. Matching the stone or other material used for the patio will integrate the design, and the patio surface itself will be easier to keep clean because soil won't overflow from the bed onto the paving. The bed can be raised as little as 6 inches or as much as 2 or 3 feet. Higher beds will be easier to work in, and if you finish the top with wide stones or boards, it will even create additional seating space.

Choosing plants that drape and billow over the sides will help to soften the hard lines of stone. A raised bed of about 2 feet will break up the perpendicularity of patio and fence (it's the same design concept as using foundation shrubs).

You can use the soil excavated from building the patio in the newly created raised bed, provided you supplement it with good-quality topsoil and compost and mix them both in well. If the border extends all the way around your patio, you may need a couple of cubic yards (see the sidebar "How Much Path Material Will You Need?" in Chapter Three). Be prepared to cart soil in the back gate or, as many gardeners in small spaces do, through the house (with the floor covered in heavy-duty plastic, of course). The soil level will settle over time and as it gets watered, but even so, don't fill the bed too full at first, so that later you can add a layer of mulch without the bed overflowing.

Plant in layers just as you would in any other bed. (Remember that the raised bed automatically adds 2 feet to the height of any plant.) A bed planted with only perennials will be dismal in winter, so use a mixed palette of plants that includes evergreen shrubs, small trees with interesting bark, early bulbs, and winter flowers. If you spend time in your patio in the winter—not unheard of in the Northwest, especially if you have a roof over the patio—this will leave you with an attractive view.

Decks

Decks are house extensions—usually attached but sometimes freestanding—that are built up off the ground. In the Northwest, there's hardly a back garden without one. Decks differ from porches, because porches are usually more integral to the architecture of the house than a deck. Porches run along the front or back of a house, sometimes turning a corner. Decks extend from the back or side of a house, and it doesn't matter if you enter them off the second-floor bedroom or the kitchen. Decks are tacked on anytime we need an outdoor area to sit.

Deck Construction

Deck construction is just that; you're building a structure that needs permit approval, appropriate construction materials, and proper footings to make sure the deck is safe and long-lasting, as well as attractive. Your local lumber or home improvement store can help with the building plans; check with your city or county's construction and land use department for permits.

Above: **This ground-level deck, extending out from the house, has built-in planters along the sides.**

Make more room in the small garden by building the deck off-center. The conventional deck is centered along the back of the house, or at least centered with the door that opens onto it. That design can give a pleasing, symmetrical feeling. But in the small garden, you may want to place the deck at an angle or on the corner of the house, to give you more open garden space. This works best if the back door (or access to the deck) is also off-center. It's an uncomfortable feeling to walk out onto a shallow landing with a tray full of dishes or burgers for the grill and have no room to negotiate a turn.

Any change of level makes a space look larger. But don't sacrifice usefulness for artifice: if you try to squeeze two deck levels in by making the deck slightly smaller, you may not be able to use the spaces you've created. In the small garden, there is usually not room for two-layered decks. Decks automatically provide you with two levels, even if it's only a few steps down to a lower part of the garden.

Above: **Changing levels creates another garden space. Here, the steps between gardens make the perfect setting for pots of annuals, including fancy-leaved pelargoniums, light- and dark-pink** *Diascia,* **and licorice plant** *(Helichrysum petiolare).*

Railings provide safety, aesthetics, or both. A deck that's close to the ground may not need a railing, but a railing can still be useful to define the space. Higher decks will need a railing for safety. Whether it's made of horizontal rails or pickets, a railing provides a visual boundary, but not a solid wall; this draws the eye out and helps to enlarge the garden instead of creating too many tiny spaces. Railings also provide another place for plants. Round planters or long, window box–style containers can be secured to the railing. Hanging containers can be wooden, plastic, or wire-framed (the last type is lined with moss or coconut fiber). Because the light surrounds planters on deck railings, the plantings in them will usually stay nicely symmetrical. If the sun hits mostly on one side, there will be more growth on that side, but the growth will still be more even than it would be in a planter against a wall.

For deck seating, measure from the back of one chair, across the table, to the back of an opposite chair. (Make sure that the chairs are pulled out a comfortable distance before you measure.) That's the minimum amount of space you need for the deck. A round table that seats four or five plus chairs will take up at least 10 feet by 10 feet. A deck with a table and chairs takes a lot of room, but you'll need more room than that. Take into your space consideration how you will move—walking around the table to get to the steps, for example. And be sure to make room for the barbecue.

Deck Materials

Here are the most common options for deck material:

■ Pressure-treated wood is probably the most popular choice. The wood is infused with chemicals that help it resist rot, keeping your creation solid and safe. Gardeners concerned about the arsenic in this wood may prefer a different material.

■ Wood that is naturally resistant, usually cedar or redwood, is also an option. These woods can be left untreated to weather to a natural gray. Redwood is a slow-growing tree that doesn't regenerate nearly as fast as cedar, and so many gardeners prefer to use cedar, a long-lasting material that doesn't deplete the environment.

■ "Plastic lumber" makes an extremely long-lasting deck. It never has to be treated or stained, you don't have to worry about anything rotting, and even the limited color choices don't matter, because once it's underfoot, it gets covered with chairs, tables, feet, and pots. One popular product (Trex) is made from 50 percent recycled wood and 50 percent recycled plastic. It can be used for decks, steps, and railings. It's easy to maintain, and doesn't get slick with moss in our wet Northwest winters.

Deck Plantings

Pots on the deck need to steer clear of winter wet. Lift them off the flooring with "pot feet," or pull them up close to the house and under the eaves during the winter. If you have the space, tip large containers onto their sides during rainy Northwest winters to keep them well drained. This is a good method for a pot of herbaceous plants, but if you have woody plants in the container, you'll need to be careful that their branches don't get broken and are not aimed to trip you up on a journey across the deck.

Use the ground at the base of the deck for more planting space. Plant a vine in the ground that can be trained up one corner of the deck. If it's vigorous enough, it can be trained along the railing (wisteria comes to mind immediately, but grapes, *Akebia*, and *Clematis montana* would also do well). A tree, grown up at the corner of the deck, could eventually provide shade for what becomes unrelenting sunshine in summer. Deciduous trees offer shade in summer and, after the leaves drop, let what winter sun there is in to warm the house.

Chapter Seven

■ Can I Go Organic in My Small Garden?

■ Can I Have a Wildlife Garden?

■ Can I Have a Water Feature?

■ Can I Have a Fruit Garden?

■ Is There Room for a Greenhouse?

■ Can I Have Chickens in My Small Garden?

■ Is There Room for Vegetables?

Left: **Small, yes, but even gardens with little room offer options and possibilities.**

Can I Do That?

Even the small garden has unused potential: nooks and crannies that can be developed, a section that can be redesigned to have a different feel, an area that suddenly would make more sense if it were turned into . . .

Instead of being limited by size, many gardeners decide on what's important to them and then do it. Consequently, there are small gardens that contain every amenity, style, and purpose that larger gardens do—although, admittedly, not all in the same place. You may have always wanted (fill in the blank here) but didn't think you had room. Consider these ideas that can easily be incorporated into the small garden.

Can I Go Organic in My Small Garden?

There are compelling reasons to go organic in the garden, and especially when you garden in a small space. There is no close contact with chemicals, and no need to waste valuable storage space on various bottles, canisters, spray equipment, and protective clothing. Many chemicals are applied by spraying, and in the small garden it is all too likely that drift will damage plants that become unintended targets. Herbicide damage to plants is a common occurrence: you treat weeds in one area, and next thing you know the camellia has yellow veins running through its green leaves.

Not only can you have an organic small garden, it is the best and really the easiest way to garden. No worry about how to suit up to spray something, no worry about what was in the sprayer the last time you used it, no concern about a spray drifting over to damage choice plants, no worry about what else is dying in the garden besides your target pest. In an organic garden, you are free to walk barefoot across your small lawn, chew on the end of a petunia to taste the sweetness, and pick a few self-seeded johnny-jump-ups to toss in a salad.

Start Organic

Just how do you do battle with the evil pests and diseases that attack your plants? Plant pathologists agree that 75 percent of plant problems stem from cultural practices. In other words, it's our fault. Make your plant decisions count, and you'll greatly reduce landscape problems.

■ Poor plant selection and poor siting are the first things that go wrong. In the Northwest, that usually means putting a full-sun plant in a shady place, but it can also mean choosing a pest-susceptible plant in the first place. Birch trees, such as the beautiful *Betula utilis* var. *jackmontii*, with its ghostly white bark, are susceptible to aphids. It's a beautiful tree, and you can accommodate it even in the small garden if you place it in a corner where its winter bark can be backlit, but your car or sidewalk doesn't get coated with sticky honeydew from aphids. Then let the aphids' predators lady bugs and bushtits, for example— have a feast.

■ Don't stress plants unduly: plant shade-lovers such as *Leucothoë* in the shade, not in a windy, sunny position.

■ Improper pruning practices of woody plants, including topping trees and heading back branches to leave a stub, are an invitation to fungal and bacterial diseases. Know how to prune, or hire a professional. Any landscape-maintenance company in the Northwest that advertises "view pruning" is veiling its true practices. Be assured that it will top the cedars and Douglas firs, causing problems more serious than a lost view of Puget Sound.

Below: **Organic gardens are full of healthy and beautiful plants. In this organic garden, a self-seeded sweet pea ('Cupani') shares space with a rose ('The Herbalist').**

Use Organic Controls

When problems do occur, look for organic controls such as the following:

■ Put up with some damage. It's a part of life in the garden to let a few caterpillars eat some leaves; otherwise, where would all the butter-flies come from?

■ Remove a plant if the damage is too severe, or move it if its site is part of the problem. Sometimes gardeners need permission to take out a plant. Now you have that permission.

■ Let the birds and good bugs eat pests. An organic garden is well rounded; we put up with the pests because we know that beneficial insects will be drawn to the garden to eat them. Parasitic wasps lay eggs on tent caterpillars; soldier beetles and lady beetles (which we call ladybugs) and their larvae consume thousands of aphids.

■ Use environmentally safe products in an environ-mentally safe way. Insecticidal soap sprays, which must be applied directly to the pests, can kill aphids without harming ladybugs. In Northwest springs, when aphids feast on new growth, it may be neces-sary to use such a spray as often as every other day.

But be aware that even some organic controls, such as those based on pyrethrum, can kill fish if they get into a stream in heavy enough concentration.

■ Control slugs by patrolling at night or in early morning with a sharp stick; set tuna cans full of cheap beer on the ground and cover with a small, upturned terra-cotta pot (for aesthetics); or sprinkle the area with a pelleted form of iron phosphate, sold by several companies under various name brands (Sluggo is one example). Many a hosta has been saved by this type of product.

■ A corn gluten product can control broadleaf evergreen weeds in lawns.

■ Horticultural oils, applied during the winter, smother the eggs and emerging larvae on many woody plants, which can be especially helpful on fruit trees (you'd like to know that what you harvest is safe to eat).

■ Use undiluted white vinegar on grass that comes up in pavement cracks and on weeds in the lawn. Pour it on directly and it kills the plant (this works best in hot, sunny weather). Or pour boiling water on the weeds.

New, safe organic remedies and preventions are being tested constantly. Ask around, or join a local garden group (or create your own) of like-minded people. Organic practices have minimal impact on the environment and help gardens, wildlife, and nature flourish.

Can I Have a Wildlife Garden?

The term "wildlife garden" might conjure up the vision of a vast meadow or woodland. But even a small garden can be inviting to birds, amphibians, and small mammals. The variety of wildlife that probably uses your garden would amaze you. Birds, butterflies, hummingbirds, squirrels, garter snakes, and possums may visit your garden or pass through it on their way to somewhere else either in the daytime or during the night.

Birds win out as the most sought after wildlife in a garden, and there are ways you can encourage them to think of your garden as their home—or at least their favorite restaurant. A garden with birds seems alive, and not only will you be entertained by the variety of birds that come to your feeders, but your plants will be healthier. In addition to the seeds we offer them, birds eat a variety of insects. Even starlings, which most people consider pests, do their part by eating the grubs (larvae) of craneflies—the bane of lawn-lovers' existence.

It should go without saying that the wildlife garden is one without chemicals. Even carefully covered slug bait containing metaldehyde can get accidentally uncovered and poison birds.

Attracting Wildlife to Your Small Garden

Above: **Called pheasant berry, the shrub** *Leycesteria formosa* **also feeds town birds, such as the chickadee.**

Here are some ways you can encourage wildlife in your small garden. For more detailed information on making your garden a backyard wildlife sanctuary, contact your state's department of fish and wildlife or your local chapter of the Audubon Society.

■ Plant more trees and shrubs. Even in the small garden, we can create layers of vegetation. Many birds like to fly from higher trees into shrubs and then to feeders. This is where you can borrow not only views but whole trees! Use your neighbor's hemlock by planting tall shrubs on that side of your property and layering with smaller shrubs closer to the feeder.

■ Evergreen plants give winter cover to small birds, helping keep them out of the way of predators such as hawks or cats, and giving them a roosting place protected from cold winds.

■ Provide water. Water is not only essential for a complete wildlife garden, it adds to the fun. A shallow birdbath is ideal, but a tray of water or a terra-cotta plant saucer on the ground can serve as a birdbath when the notion strikes. Little birds splash and drink, and they also like to take "showers." You can watch them gather when a larger bird, such as a robin, goes to the birdbath. As the robin splashes wildly, the little birds sit on the rim, enjoying the water spray. Once you've observed this, you may even want to provide a more complex birdbath for your winged denizens: a fountain with either a constant or a timed spray would be a big hit.

■ Provide a variety of feeders—hanging, table, suet—and you'll be rewarded with a variety of birds. Even small city gardens can draw Steller's jays (a showy Western species common in Northwest cities and towns) and flickers (woodpecker relatives). Make sure some of your shrubs and trees have berries in the winter. In the small garden, we need to have ornament all year round, and the fruit will provide food for many kinds of birds. Even robins, who usually prefer to look for worms, will take advantage of berried bushes in late winter when food sources are scarce. Fruits of such plants as *Cotoneaster,* hawthorn, pyracantha, and crabapples increase in sugar as they ripen, aided by cold weather. It's a joy to watch a flock of birds, in the weeks after Christmas, feed on fruit while enlivening the leafless branches.

■ Hummingbirds are drawn to brightly colored flowers (reds and yellows), particularly those with funnel shapes (just right for those long beaks to dive into). Many hummingbird plants are perfect for small gardens. Plant salvias, penstemons, and fuchsias in pots and containers on decks and balconies. A sugar/water feeder will keep them coming (no need to add food coloring), and you'll be amazed at how much of a show they put on. Be sure to thoroughly wash the feeder weekly.

■ Place toad houses in the garden (toads eat slugs), and leave small rock piles for garter snakes (ditto).

■ Even possums, those nocturnal visitors to urban gardens everywhere, can help. Not only do they not carry nasty diseases, they too eat slugs in the garden. Bon appétit!

Can I Have a Water Feature?

No need to dismiss ponds and fountains as fit only for large gardens. There is a type or style of water feature for every size garden, and there is room for water in any small garden—indeed, water is especially valuable there. Still water is a mirror, making the small garden larger. And the sound of moving water brings life into the garden, whether it trickles, bubbles, or pours.

■ Create a water garden in a half oak barrel (liners are made to that specific size), and plant a small water lily, such as *Nymphaea tetragona* 'Helvola'.

■ If you dig a pond, call the city first to find out where the utilities and sewer lines are.

■ Site the water garden in a sunny place, but be sure to provide a shady corner where fish can cool off (a rocky overhang will do).

■ Buy a preformed liner in a shape and size appropriate to your pond site. Dig a hole slightly wider than the shape, and when you've put the liner in, fill in the remaining space between liner and soil.

Below: **Whether it be a formal built-in pool or a lined whiskey barrel, a water feature is easy to include in the small garden.**

■ Or build your pond to suit. Rubber or PVC pond lining, which is thick and resistant to tearing, can be bought in any length and in several different widths (for example, 5, 10, or 15 feet). Dig your hole a few inches deeper than you need and add some sand at the bottom; this is so that no sharp rocks, roots, etc. will stick up and pierce the liner (you can even use a piece of old carpet). Then place the lining. Secure it with stones around the edge and start to fill with water, removing or rearranging the stones as the liner sinks. The edging left around the top of the pond will help stop leaks; when you landscape with flat stones it will be disguised.

■ Build a formal fountain. The straight lines of a formal raised water feature built from brick have a classic look, and this shape may allow you more planting area in the small garden. As with any straight edges, the feature

Above: **The natural look of this small pond comes from the use of water plants, such as variegated flag (Iris pseudacorus 'Variegata'), and nearby plants, such as the Japanese blood grass (Imperata cylindrica 'Red Baron'), which only looks as if it is sitting in wet soil.**

can be softened by water plants or by a fountain. Fountains come with various sounds, so choose what you want to hear. A fountain that overflows into a larger container has a soft, burbling sound. A clear, pouring sound comes from a wall fountain as the stream hits the water below. Small, cascading waterfalls lend the illusion that you're high in the mountains

■ Choose plants for the water's edge and for submerging in the pond. Cardinal flower *(Lobelia cardinalis), Rodgersia,* Japanese primroses *(Primula japonica),* and rushes (such as the curly *Juncus effusus* 'Spiralis') would do well around the damp edges of a pond. Water lilies, water lettuce *(Pistia stratiotes),* and pickerel weed *(Pontederia cordata)* prefer to be submerged. Water hyacinth *(Eichhornia crassipes),* a popular pond plant, is highly invasive if let loose in our waterways. This happens when gardeners drain ponds into existing streams, so be careful if you choose this plant.

■ Many water plants prefer still water, so you may need to decide between a fountain and plants (larger ponds can have quiet corners and edges). If you opt for a fountain, you can still plant marginal water plants—those that like soil wet but don't need to be in standing water— around the edges.

■ Use a submersible pump for moving water. Pumps are available in many sizes, some suitable for tiny tabletop fountains and others for larger landscape pools. They recirculate the water, so that you only need to top it off occasionally. (Higher humidity and cool temperatures slow water evaporation; low humidity and high temperatures quicken it.) For water action in the pond, you'll need to run electricity out to the site. But in the small garden, that isn't far.

■ Include fish in your pond. An area as small as 3 feet across and 18 inches deep is big enough for a few goldfish, but for koi, 24 inches deep is better. A good filtration system can make up for a lack of space. Talk to a koi specialist as you make your pond plans.

Can I Have a Small Fruit Garden?

To look at the size of some old apple trees, you'd think you would have no garden left if you planted one. But, fortunately, there are many choices of fruit trees and shrubs for the small garden that will still leave you room for other plants and a place to sit.

You may need to use up most or all of your sunniest spots for fruit, but is that so bad? Not only are you able to harvest fruit from your trees and shrubs, but they provide an ornamental aspect in themselves. Apple blossoms are the epitome of springtime; the aroma of ripening fruit speaks of fall; and the fiery autumn tones of blueberry foliage can go up against those of the best maple.

For fruit in the small garden, choose from among these trees and shrubs:

■ Apples are available on mini-dwarf or dwarf rootstock. Trees grafted onto these rootstocks may grow from a mere 6 to 12 feet, although their ultimate size depends on how vigorous a grower the grafted variety is. Mini-dwarf trees are small enough so that you may be able to fit several into a small garden, and they grow well in large containers (such as half oak barrels).

■ Columnar apple trees grow straight and narrow, like a beanpole. With no side branches, the spurs (the short stems that bear flowers and fruit) come right off the main stem. These trees grow to about 7 feet and easily fit into a container on the deck or patio.

■ Espaliered trees can also fit into the small garden. To espalier a tree or shrub is to train it into a two-dimensional form, such as a fan or a cordon (straight horizontal branches coming off a main stem). This creates a beautiful display of flowers and fruit, and makes picking that much easier. Espaliered trees grow well against a wall or fence, but sometimes freestanding espaliers can be used as a fence themselves (see "Elegant Espalier for Walls and Fences" in Chapter Four).

Below: **Lending a Mediterranean look to this porch, the Meyer lemon can be left out most of the year and kept in a bright window during winter.**

■ If you want dwarf cherry trees, choose ones that have been grafted onto what is called Gisela (or Giessen) rootstock. This keeps the trees to a manageable size of 8 to 10 feet tall. You can grow and enjoy sweet or tart cherries on these small trees (the list of available varieties is long), which are also resistant to many of the usual cherry diseases. Cherries, like apples, set fruit better if there are two different plants that bloom at the same time. Most nursery catalogs have charts that show which variety goes best with which.

■ Don't stop with just a fruit tree. Blueberries—usually wide shrubs to 6 feet tall—can be grown in containers provided you choose dwarf varieties such as 'Northsky' and 'North Country'. Blueberries, too, set fruit better with two varieties present.

■ More unconventionally, you can grow ornamental plants that have the bonus of good-tasting fruit. The Northwest native evergreen huckleberry *(Vaccinium ovatum)* not only makes a wonderful, informal hedge to 4 feet but bears sweet black fruit—and will even set fruit in part shade.

■ There's always room for strawberries. Luscious fruit can be had from a few square feet. Don't use the terra-cotta "strawberry pots," which have pockets around the sides into which you tuck several plants. They're attractive, and the fruit stays off the ground and clean, but the pots dry out so quickly in warm weather that you may not be able to keep up with the needs of the developing crop.

■ Grow a strawberry that is ornamental as well as good to eat. *Fragaria vesca,* the alpine strawberry, was grown as a delicacy in France 200 years ago. The plants spread by underground stems to form a good ground cover, without being aggressive. They take sun or part shade, and flower and fruit all spring, summer, and into the fall, producing small but sweet berries. A few of these plants will give you enough fruit to gather in the mornings for your cereal (it'll also get you out for an early stroll in the garden). 'Rugen' and 'Alpine Yellow' are two cultivars sold.

■ Plant a lemon tree—even in the Northwest. 'Improved Meyer' is a dwarf well suited for a container on the deck that can be easily moved into your sunny window for the winter (lemon trees winter outdoors only in warm climates). Meyer lemon has glossy, dark green leaves, fragrant, waxy white flowers, and fruit throughout the year. Meyer lemons are juicy and tasty, with a lower acidity than commercial varieties.

Is There Room for a Greenhouse?

Even a balcony garden can accommodate some of the small-space greenhouses on the market today, allowing you to start seedlings, overwinter tender plants, and root cuttings. The smallest houses are the ones that you can't walk into; they have three or four shelves and are three-sided, to fit up against the wall of your house or apartment. They hold at least nine flats, and that's quite a few plants for your garden. Walk-in greenhouses come as small as 6 feet by 8 feet, and some have sliding entries so you don't need the room to swing open a door. A greenhouse attached to the back or side wall of your house or condominium can be almost like a conservatory; if you can fit a chair inside, think how lovely your cup of coffee will be on winter mornings. Regardless, the "lean-to" saves on energy if it covers a door to the inside: it will help warm up indoors on a sunny winter day.

Portable greenhouses, which use light plastic sheeting to cover the frame, are available, but they tend to look like big plastic bags flapping in the wind. In the small garden there's no place to hide one of these, so it's better to build something more permanent that also looks good. Set up your greenhouse to maximize its potential:

■ Greenhouses need to be sited in the sun so that your tomato seedlings can get off to the best start. If possible, place the structure with the long side running east and west, to catch the most winter and spring sun. Place the greenhouse on the south side of your property if possible.

■ Monitor the inside temperature and provide vents. If you run an outdoor extension cord to the greenhouse, you can have light, heat, automatic vents, and a fan.

■ Temperature control can be set on a timer, so that it won't get too cold in winter or too hot in summer. Winter temperatures may not be a problem because the shelter itself can cut the cold and add several degrees of protection. Seeds sown in early spring can warm up during the sunny days and won't mind some cooling at night. In the summer, if you prefer to go low-tech, keep an eye on the thermometer and open the door and vents yourself to create a cooling breeze.

You'll find that, even in the smallest greenhouse, you can grow more flower or vegetable starts than you need. Plan on swapping, giving away, or donating plants to a local sale (you know, it's really difficult to plant only three tomato seeds).

Below: **Starting your own seeds of annuals and vegetables is not only economical but rewarding. Greenhouses are available in sizes (6 feet by 8 feet; 8 feet by 8 feet) that fit into small gardens.**

Can I Have Chickens in My Small Garden?

Some gardeners long for a little bit of country in the city. Chickens provide fresh eggs (chicks bought in spring should start laying at age six months); they also will eat bugs, and you can toss them weeds you've pulled. And they're great at turning over compost for you as they scratch around. Most municipalities will count chickens as they do other domesticated animals. If the limit is three animals per household, then you could have two chickens and a cat, three chickens, or one chicken and two dogs (although one chicken can be a lonely figure).

Chickens need:

■ A minimum of 16 square feet of space each

■ A place to roost (a few feet off the ground)

■ A safe, enclosed place to lay their eggs (the nest box)

■ A henhouse, which is a place to sleep undisturbed by marauding raccoons (they really do "go to bed" every night)

■ A dusty corner for a "bath" (it keeps the mites down)

■ A constant supply of water

■ Feed (in addition to the weeds that you toss them)

Below: **Check with your municipality for regulations on keeping chickens. Many cities allow up to three animals per household, which includes cats, dogs, and chickens.**

Chickens can live happily in an enclosed run as long as they have enough room. You can build a portable coop that looks like a tall, long triangle (plans for the age-old design, often called a chicken tiller, are available in books and from your local extension service). Place the chicken coop in a part-shade area of the garden, or alongside the garage.

Providing clean litter at the bottom of the coop will make it easy to clean out, and what you rake out can be composted to provide organic matter and nutrients to the garden. Use shredded landscape material (that mix of chips, twigs, and leaves) or spread peat around.

It should go without saying that roosters are not a great idea in the small city garden. You might not mind their early wake-up call, but your neighbors may be on a different schedule.

Is There Room for Vegetables?

Gone are the days of the estate kitchen garden, where you had to walk away from the house and into a walled area to cut the lettuce or pick tomatoes. Then, no one wanted to see the food actually growing. Today's vegetable gardens are often in full view and within easy reach.

Find the sunniest part of your garden. This might be along the south-facing side of the house (the house reflects and radiates heat, which is what tomatoes, peppers, and eggplants need). You can turn the sunny front garden into your own vegetable patch.

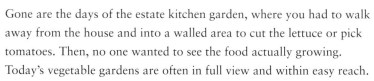

Below: **Even rampant growers such as this 'Sun Gold' cherry tomato can fit into the small garden—if you love it enough, you'll find room.**

Don't grow edibles among the ornamentals. This is all the rage—at least in theory. The reality is that many vegetables start out looking pretty but eventually look either trussed up or so picked over you'd think an army of slugs had been at work. Lettuce comes in attractive shades, from bright spring green to mahogany, but continual harvesting by removing individual leaves or cutting the whole head and letting the plant resprout gives the ornamental garden a devastated appearance. On top of that, vegetables need attention with water and fertilizer that ornamental plants don't and shouldn't get.

Plant edible flowers among the lettuce and zucchini—calendulas, pansies (especially the cute little johnny-jump-ups), and borage offer color in the garden and in your salads. Use two or three lavender plants to give that feeling of an acre-sized English kitchen garden—but plant them at the edge, since lavender doesn't want or need the water and fertilizer that your crops do.

Grow vegetables in containers. Container vegetable gardens are easy and convenient, and they needn't take up much space; on a west- or southwest-facing balcony, you could fit in several pots for food.

Here are some vegetable varieties suited to small gardens and containers:

■ Tomatoes—'Tumbler' and 'Patio' grow well in containers or hanging baskets; even the larger plants of other cherry tomatoes can fit if you want them enough.

■ Peppers—'Jingle Bells' is a sweet variety that stays small and works well in a container; 'Habañero' is a hot choice.

■ Eggplants—'Bambino' produces walnut-sized fruit.

■ Cucumbers—smaller-growing varieties such as 'Fanfare' can be trained on a small trellis.

■ Summer squash are usually too rambunctious for containers, but nonvining varieties can fit into the small kitchen garden. Described as compact, these plants can still reach a good 4 feet across; look for bush varieties.

■ Pole beans can grow up an arbor or a trellis; they take up more vertical space than horizontal. Grow an old variety such as 'Scarlet Runner' or 'Painted Lady' and you'll have pretty flowers and something to eat.

■ Bush beans can be grown in containers.

■ Greens mixes, such as the French mesclun, can be sown in a pot and trimmed regularly for salads, as can lettuce. Sow successive pots of lettuce (every two weeks throughout the spring) and you can change them out, always having a fresh supply on hand. In mild Northwest winters, lettuce and greens can be grown late into the fall and started early in the spring. If sun is at a premium, you can plant lettuce in a place that gets some afternoon shade, provided it gets full sun the rest of the day. Lettuce is about the only vegetable that will put up with shade.

Grow herbs in containers on a sunny balcony, deck, or patio. (Don't bother trying an indoor herb garden—there is never enough sun.) Most herbs, including rosemary, sage, thyme, and oregano, are of Mediterra-nean origin; they like it bright and hot, and they don't want any coddling. Basil can be seeded out in a container in June and by mid-July you'll be able to start harvesting (give the whole pot a "haircut"). Because it's an annual that produces big leaves fast, basil needs attention with regular water and fertilizer that other herbs don't need or want.

- ■ **Grasses**
- ■ **Ground Covers and Edgers**
- ■ **Hedges**
- ■ **Narrow Plants**
- ■ **Perennials**
- ■ **Shrubs**
- ■ **Small Conifers**
- ■ **Trees**
- ■ **Varigated Plants**
- ■ **Vines and Climbers**

Left: **Plants that are carefully chosen for the small garden can create a well-orchestrated, year-long show.**

Plant Lists

"Choose wisely" should be the motto of plant selection in the small garden. Thoughtful selection (coupled with, to be honest, some impulse buying) results in a small garden where healthy plants put on a show all year long. Use the following plant lists as guides; they are filled with plant ideas for particular situations (narrow places, hedges), structure (trees, shrubs), flowers (perennials), and foliage (small conifers, variegated plants). Choose from a list of plants that grow low (ground covers) and plants that grow up (vines). In other words, there are plants for every inch of the small garden.

Consider well-drained soil a requirement for all plants unless otherwise stated. Zones refer to the USDA Hardiness Zone Map.

Grasses

Grasses are superb plants for the small garden because they have at least three seasons of interest. They add movement and fine texture, and they often have both lovely fall color and fine winter form. So many different grasses are available today that it's easy to choose sun or shade, wide leaves or narrow, arching or upright, and variegated, blue, or green leaves. That's in addition to height: You can find sizes ranging from tiny tufts of grass no bigger than 6 inches to plumes rising to 8 feet.

We tend to think of grasses as being dry-soil plants. Some indeed do well in dry soils, but many others prefer regular water in dry spells, and still others do best in dampish sites.

Evergreen grasses add a spark to winter gardens and containers, and many are hardy in the Northwest. Deciduous grasses can age to fine shades of straw or gold in winter, and may hold together until well after Christmas before they need to be cut back to make room for new growth.

Choose grasses that fit into the planting scheme, rather than those that will overwhelm nearby plants. And if reseeding worries you—a few choice grasses have a tendency to spread themselves around—be vigilant about cutting off flower stalks before they set seed.

Below: **Comfortable companions: A 'Heritage' rose peaks out from *Carex morrowii* 'Variegata'.**

NAME	APPEARANCE	CULTURE	NOTES
Calamagrostis x *acutiflora* 'Overdam' (feather reed grass)	Deciduous upright growth to 4 ft. including flower stalks; silver-veined leaves.	Part shade. Zone 5	Narrow grass for a shady nook. Combine with a cultivar of the low-growing *Rhododendron yakushimanum*, such as 'Bashful', to 1 ft. with pink flowers.
Calamagrostis x *acutiflora* 'Karl Foerster' (feather reed grass)	Deciduous to 5 ft. including flower stalks; narrow-growing, to only 18 in. wide.	Sun or part shade. Zone 5	Fit one into a tight place or use three for stronger impact. This and the previous cultivar are sterile hybrids, so they won't reseed.
Carex buchananii (leatherleaf sedge)	Copper-bronze upright foliage with pigtail curl at end; 2 to 3 ft.	Full sun to part shade; dry summer soil OK. Zone 7	Show off its unusual color next to a small evergreen shrub such as *Quercus sadleriana*; works in large containers too.
Carex dolichostachys 'Kaga-nishiki' (goldfountains)	Evergreen clumps of foliage to 15 in. high and as wide; narrow leaves edged in gold.	Full sun or part shade; takes dry soil in shade. Zone 5	A bright accent for a shady spot; good for a pot; spreads extremely slowly by clumps.
Carex morrowii 'Ice Dance' (Ice Dance variegated sedge) and 'Variegata'	Evergreen clumps of foliage to 1 ft. high and as wide; wide leaves edged in creamy white. Thin white stripes run down leaves of 'Variegata'.	Part shade to shade; takes dry soil in shade. Zone 6	Bold statement on a small plant; year-round tidy appearance makes it perfect for entry gardens and display containers in winter; spreads in a tight fashion by clumps.
Carex ornithopoda 'Variegata' (bird's-foot sedge)	Evergreen clumps to only 6 in.; yellow stripe down the middle of each leaf.	Full sun or part shade. Zone 5	Good edger; diminutive but bright color draws the eye down.
Carex testacea (orange sedge)	Evergreen clump to 2 ft.; narrow leaves green with copper tint in summer, turning bright orange on top in winter.	Full sun; takes dry soil. Zone 6	Accent winter color by combining with bright foliage of heathers such as apricot-toned *Calluna* 'Blazeaway'.
Deschampsia caespitosa 'Northern Lights' (Northern Lights tufted grass)	Evergreen to 1 ft. high and as wide; creamy variegated foliage, new growth blushed pink; flower stalks to 15 in.	Full sun to part shade. Zone 5	Nice in containers where it can flow over the edge; plant with pink flowers to bring out highlights.
Hakonechloa macra 'Aureola' (golden variegated Japanese forest grass)	Deciduous, Lax mound of foliage to 1 ft. high and 3 ft. across; leaves variegated with gold.	Part shade. Zone 5	Tumbles like water over rocks, down a shallow slope, or over the side of a container; yellow-tan winter look is OK, but cut it back mid- to late winter.
Helictotrichon sempervirens (blue oat grass)	Evergreen clumps to 2 ft. high (4 ft. including early-summer flower stalks) and as wide; foliage blue-gray, stiff to fountainlike.	Full sun; dry soil OK. Zone 5	Give it a tough spot and it shines. Don't cut down; in late winter, groom foliage by pulling a rake or hand cultivator through to get dead leaves out. A moderate but not annoying reseeder.

NAME	APPEARANCE	CULTURE	NOTES
Miscanthus sinensis 'Adagio' (Adagio maiden hair grass)	Deciduous clumps up to 3 ft.; plumes in late summer.	Full sun. Zone 5	Miniature version of maiden grass. The cultivar 'Yaku Jima' reaches 4 ft.
M. sinensis 'Gracilimus' (maiden grass)	Deciduous clump to 5 ft. high; foliage turns golden in fall.	Full sun. Zone 5	Medium to tall, so remember that small plants beneath it will be covered in fountains of foliage. Cut down mid- to late winter.
M. sinensis 'Morning Light' (Morning Light maiden grass)	Deciduous to 4 ft. high and 3 ft. wide; silver-edged leaves; late-summer flower stalks just above foliage.	Full sun. Zone 5	Medium-sized maiden grass; variegated foliage adds shimmery effect. Cut down mid- to late winter.
M. sinensis 'Strictus' (porcupine grass)	Deciduous clumps to 6 ft. (8 ft. with flowers); unusual horizontal banding in yellow.	Full sun. Zone 5	More narrow-growing than 'Zebrinus'. This full-sized grass needs space, so don't crowd it (also, you want to see the odd variegation).
M. sinensis 'Zebrinus' (zebra grass)	Deciduous clumps to 6 ft. (8 ft. with flowers); unusual horizontal banding in yellow.	Full sun. Zone 5	Almost like 'Strictus', although some gardeners find this one develops into wider clump.
Molinia caerulea 'Variegata' (variegated moor grass)	Deciduous clumps to 15 in. high and as wide; foliage variegated creamy white.	Full sun. Zone 5	A shining clump, and small enough to be part of the garden, not the whole show. Cut down in late winter.
Panicum virgatum 'Heavy Metal' (blue switch grass)	Deciduous, columnar growth to 5 ft.; blue-gray foliage.	Full sun. Zone 4	Colorful grass without the bulk of some. 'Haense Herms' 4 ft., red fall foliage; 'Rehbraun' 3 ft., red-brown in fall; 'Rotstrahlbusch' 4 ft., red-mahogany in fall.
Pennisetum alopecuroides 'Hameln' (dwarf fountain grass)	Deciduous mounds to 2 ft. high and as wide; white bottlebrush-like blooms in summer.	Full sun; dry soil OK. Zone 6	Grassy, flowing effect. Cut down in late winter. 'Little Bunny' to 18 in.; 'Moudry' to 3 ft., blackish flowers.
Stipa gigantea (giant feather grass)	Deciduous clump; foliage to 18 in. but flower stalks to 6 ft.	Full sun. Zone 7	Giant flower stalks make a stunning contrast with low-to-the-ground foliage.
Stipa tenuissima (Mexican feather grass)	Deciduous to 2 ft.; light green growth turns blonde in summer.	Full sun. Zone 6	Blink and it's reseeded all over the place, but its "golden waves of grain" look in the wind makes it worthwhile. Also listed as *Nassella tenuissima*.

Ground Covers and Edgers

Ground covers provide the lowest layer of plants in the garden, contributing to lush, multilevel plantings. Dense growers can suppress weeds, either by forming a mat or by shading the ground so that weed seeds don't germinate. (This isn't a surefire thing, so don't be surprised if you still have to pull a few weeds even after the ground-cover plant is established.)

Choose evergreen ground covers for areas of the garden you see all winter. This is especially important in the many parts of the Northwest that don't get appreciable snow cover. Semi-evergreen and deciduous ground covers are good for disguising the dying foliage of bulbs.

Edging plants fill in the nooks and crannies of the garden. They are particularly useful around stepping-stones, between pavers, in rockeries, and along walkways. Any straight line made by sidewalk or fence is softened by the addition of a few edging plants.

Below: **In a shady location, redwood sorrel** *(Oxalis oregana)* **will do just what it is supposed to do—cover the ground.**

NAME	APPEARANCE	CULTURE	NOTES
Alchemilla ellenbeckii (lady's mantle)	Mat-forming evergreen 2 in. high and 12 in. wide; tiny leaves and red stems.	Sun or part shade; doesn't like to dry out. Zone 6	Charming, but sometimes hard to keep going as solid ground cover; still, mixes well with others. *A. alpina* has silver-rimmed leaves; clumper, makes good edger.
Armeria maritima (thrift)	Tight, small hummocks of grassy foliage, 8 in. high and 10 in. wide; pink lollipop flowers in spring and sporadically through summer.	Full sun. Zone 3	Excellent edger because it doesn't wander off. 'Dusseldorf Pride' has deep rose flowers; 'Bloodstone' has deep red flowers.
Asarum caudatum (wild ginger)	Evergreen to 6 in. high and spreading; heart-shaped leaves; odd, hard-to-see maroon flowers with 3-cornered "mouse tails."	Shade; mulch well or water regularly. Zone 7	Soft, lush look for woodland walk or shady corner.
Campanula cochlearifolia (fairies' thimbles)	Mat-forming spreader to 1 ft.; light blue flowers throughout summer.	Full sun or part shade. Zone 6	Good filler that flowers constantly. Dalmation bellflower *(C. portenschlagiana)* (Zone 5) is similar, with lavender flowers; it takes dry soil.
Cornus canadensis (bunchberry)	Deciduous to only a few inches high and spreading; white flowers in spring followed by small clusters of red berries.	Part shade to shade; prefers humusy soil. Zone 3	May be difficult to establish, but once it takes hold, you'll be charmed. Grow it in a woodland area with limbed-up, protective shrubs overhead.
Cotula squalida (brass buttons)	Evergreen, mat-forming; 2 in. high and spreading; foliage like tiny fern fronds; small "brass button" flowers in spring.	Full sun to part shade. Zone 8	Also listed as *Leptinella*. Good grass substitute that never needs mowing; will creep around stepping stones. *C. perpusilla* is similar but with bronze cast; *C. squalida* 'Platt's Black' has dark tints.
Cyclamen hederifolium (hardy cyclamen)	Mottled foliage fall through winter, dies down in summer; autumn flowers in shades of pink.	Part shade to shade. Zone 6	Buy plants instead of corms so the squirrels will leave them alone. Fabulous easy-care slow ground cover under trees and shrubs. *C. coum* blooms in winter.
Dianthus (pinks)	8 in. high and 1 ft. wide; variously blue-gray foliage with long, needlelike leaves; fragrant flowers in late spring.	Full sun; prefers lime soil so does well near concrete steps or walls; will take dry soil in summer. Zone 5 or 6	Great edger, but don't step on it. 'Crimson Treasure' has red-velvet flowers flecked with pink; 'Sops in Wine' is claret-colored.

NAME	APPEARANCE	CULTURE	NOTES
Erodium reichardii (cranesbill)	Deciduous with tiny geranium look; 6 in. high and 1 ft. wide; pink flowers spring through fall.	Full sun or part shade. Zone 8	Edger or rock garden plant; small, so use one as accent, or several for more impact.
Epimedium x *rubrum* (bishop's hat)	Evergreen heart-shaped leaves; 10 in. high and as wide; small pink flowers in clusters on 1-ft. stems in early spring.	Part shade to shade, sun in cool areas; takes dry soil. Zone 5	Plant under deciduous trees or shrubs—can scorch in hot sun. *E.* x *versicolor* 'Sulphureum' has yellow flowers.
Euonymus fortunei (winter creeper)	Evergreen, trailing/ mounding; 4 to 5 in. high, spreading 2 ft.	Full sun to part shade. Zone 5	Drape over stones or let creep around. 'Kewensis' has tiny leaves.
Fragaria chiloensis (sand strawberry)	Evergreen; glossy green leaves and red stems; to 4 in. high; spreads by creeping; may bear white flowers and edible fruit (seedy).	Full sun to part shade; dry summer soil OK. Zone 5	Easy, nonaggressive ground cover that looks neat all year; snip off plantlets that are in the way to replant elsewhere. Other ornamental strawberries: 'Pink Panda' has pink flowers; 'Lipstick' has red ones.
Geranium macrorrhizum (bigroot geranium)	Evergreen to semi-evergreen; 1 ft. high, spreading 3 ft.; aromatic felted leaves take on red tints in cold weather; pink flowers in late spring.	Full sun to part shade; dry soil OK. Zone 5	Excellent mounding ground cover with billowing growth that softens the hard lines of paths.
Gypsophila repens 'Rosea' (creeping baby's breath)	Deciduous, airy growth 4 in. high and 2 ft. wide; pink flowers early through midsummer.	Full sun; takes dry soil OK. Zone 4 or 5	Use as ground cover and also over rocks and walls. Shear back in late winter for fresh growth. 'Alba' has white flowers.
Hebe pinguifolia 'Pagei' (Pagei hebe)	Evergreen gray foliage 8 in. high and 1 ft. wide; small clusters of white flowers in summer.	Full sun. Zone 6	Excellent ground cover for front of border. Shear back spent flowers for neat look (or leave them—new growth covers them up).
Hosta 'Blue Cadet' 'Golden Tiara'	Deciduous, clump-forming; both are small (to 1 ft.); flower stems to 2 ft. high; spreading to 2 ft.; blue foliage.	Part shade to shade; dry soil OK once established. Zone 5	Use a few as edgers or plant en masse as ground cover.
Lamium galeobdolon 'Hermann's Pride' (Hermann's Pride dead nettle)	Semi-evergreen clumper 1 ft. high and as wide; silver-veined leaves with bright yellow flowers along upright stems.	Part shade to shade, takes dry soil. Zone 5	Excellent edger or ground cover for shade—lights up a dark spot, and it doesn't run. Cut back completely in late winter for cleaner spring growth.

NAME	APPEARANCE	CULTURE	NOTES
Lamium maculatum (dead nettle)	Deciduous spreader to 8 in. high and 3 ft. wide; most kinds have white stripe in middle of leaf.	Part shade to shade. Zone 5	Not rampant, but you still may want to contain it in an area bordered by pavers or sidewalk. 'White Nancy' has white flowers, 'Pink Nancy' pink, 'Beacon Silver' lilac-pink.
Landscape roses *(Rosa):* Carefree series; Simplicity series; Flower Carpet series; Meidiland series	Deciduous low shrubs; all variously growing 2 to 3 ft. high and spreading 3 to 4 ft.; some continuous flowering.	Full sun, as for roses. Zones 4–5	These make fine tall ground cover to fill in sunny spots; no deadheading required. Good disease resistance for roses.
Lavandula angustifolia 'Martha Roderick' 'Blue Cushion' (lavender)	Semi-evergreen subshrubs 12 to 16 in. high and as wide; gray-green foliage; flowers in early summer to late summer; foliage and flowers aromatic.	Full sun; dry soil with sharp drainage. Zone 6	Line walks with these for a small-scale imitation of the lavender walks in England. A haircut after bloom will promote new foliage to neaten mounds.
Liriope 'Silver Midget' (Silver Midget lily turf)	Evergreen clumps of foliage to 6 in.; leaves striped white; spikes of lavender flowers.	Part shade to shade; dry soil OK. Zone 6	Great edger along a path where it can act as runway lights.
Mazus reptans	Semi-evergreen to evergreen creeper 2 in. high and 1 ft. wide; tiny blue flowers in late spring.	Full sun to part shade; may fade without some fertilizer. Zone 3	Delicate looking, but takes foot traffic, so it's good between stepping-stones.
Microbiota decussata (Siberian cypress)	Evergreen prostrate conifer to about 1 ft. high and 3 ft. wide; midgreen foliage turns bronze in winter.	Part shade; sharp drainage. Zone 3	Excellent ground cover for shallow slope; much better looking than junipers.
Oxalis oregana (redwood sorrel)	Semi-evergreen to evergreen mound to 10 in.; spreading by underground rhizomes; spring and summer flowers various shades of pink.	Part shade to shade; humusy soil; takes dryness in summer. Zone 7	Will compete with other plants, yet a lovely woodland ground cover with soft look. If foliage remains over winter, cut back before spring for fresh growth.
Pachysandra procumbens (Allegheny spurge)	Semi-evergreen 6 to 12 in. high; foliage mottled blue-green; spreads by under-ground runners; small, terminal spikes of white flowers in spring.	Shade. Zone 5	Forms a lovely carpet of green but looks terrible in sun; will grow among tree roots.
Paxistima canbyi (mountain lover)	Evergreen; 1 ft. high and 3 ft. wide; small leaves; roots where branches touch the ground.	Sun to part shade. Zone 4	Edger, accent, or container plant; plant more than one so it doesn't get overwhelmed. *P. myrsinites* (Oregon box), a Northwest native to 3 ft., is rare in cultivation.

NAME	APPEARANCE	CULTURE	NOTES
Pratia pedunculata (blue star creeper)	Semi-evergreen mat-former, 3 in. high, spreading 1 ft.; tiny leaves like baby's tears; covered in sky-blue flowers in late spring.	Full sun to part shade. Zone 7	Charming around stepping-stones or planted to resemble a streambed. Needs little maintenance except to cut back worn edges.
Raoulia australis	Evergreen, granite-colored, flat spreader; flowers insignificant.	Full sun; sharp drainage. Zone 7	Looks a bit like undulating concrete, but effective in small areas and around stepping-stones.
Saxifraga x *urbium* (London pride)	Evergreen, tight rosettes, slightly succulent; 6 in. high, spreading 1 ft. or more; sprays of light pink flowers in spring.	Part shade. Zone 6	Old-fashioned plant, but useful and attractive; good edger, or use to fill in small spaces between walk and house.
Sedum spurium (stonecrop)	Evergreen succulent 1 to 2 in. high; spreading 1 ft.; pink flowers in summer.	Full sun with sharp drainage. Zone 3	Short filler that comes in varieties with purple leaves and red flowers ('Dragon's Blood') and variegated green, cream, and pink leaves ('Tricolor').
Thymus pseudo-lanuginosus (woolly thyme)	Evergreen mat-forming spreader to 2 ft.; gray-green leaves, lavender flowers in late spring.	Full sun with sharp drainage; dry soil OK. Zone 5	Excellent edger; flowers draw bees. Other ornamental thymes for same purpose include creeping thyme *(T. serphyllum)* with red-purple flowers and tiny-leaved *T. serphyllum* 'Minus'.
Tiarella cordifolia (foamflower)	Semi-evergreen perennial with large lobed leaves and stems of white or pink foamy flowers spring through fall; 1 ft. high, 1 to 2 ft. wide, spreading slowly.	Part shade to shade. Zone 5	Valuable woodland ground cover with many selections. 'Iron Butterfly' and 'Inkspot' have dark centers to leaves; 'Ninja' has pink flowers and purple winter foliage. Cut back old leaves in late winter.
Vancouveria hexandra (inside-out flower)	Herbaceous, up to 1 ft. high and spreading; wiry stems; white flowers with swept-back petals.	Part shade. Zone 7	Make it part of the woodland collection with *Cornus canadensis* and *Asarum caudatum*.

Hedges

Hedges and screens provide much-needed privacy—or at least the idea of it—where we live elbow to elbow or where there is a particular building, road, or bus stop to camouflage. But many plants that are often chosen for hedges grow as wide as they do high, and in a small garden we are reluctant to give up a depth of 20 feet.

Fortunately, many plants are available that grow to a reasonable height and grow out only a few feet. These plants, many of them conifers, can grow until they nestle up against each other at the base, but don't necessarily grow together at the top because of their slightly pyramidal growth habits. They form an elegant, neat row, and can be used for an 8-foot space as well as a hedge the length of the property.

Hedges do not always have to be evergreen. A deciduous hedge forms a thicket of stems and twigs that, in winter, offer their own attraction. Deciduous hedges are useful where you need to screen off something only during the warm months (a deck or patio that's much used in summer may be all but abandoned in winter). The extra sun that gets through the bare branches in winter provides much-needed light at a dark time of year.

In general, create a hedge by spacing the plants 2 to 4 feet apart. The exact distance will depend more on the plant you choose than on how quickly you want it to fill in. You'll be causing problems in the long run if you try to squeeze three plants into a 4-foot space; eventually one will be crowded out and decline, and then you'll have a hole.

Informal hedges—in which shrubs are left unsheared—are more likely to offer flowers and fruit, and the forms of some shrubs have a beauty that is a shame to trim off.

Below: **Pacific wax myrtle (Myrical californica) is a tough but attractive hedge plant**.

NAME	APPEARANCE	CULTURE	NOTES
Carpinus betulus 'Frans Fontaine' (Frans Fontaine European hornbeam)	Deciduous tree 30 ft. high and 15 ft. wide; tight, regular form.	Full sun. Zone 5	Forms a thicket; can be trimmed for formal hedge. Good for letting winter sun through.
Choisya ternata (Mexican orange)	Evergreen mounding shrub 5 ft. high and as wide; fragrant white flowers in spring and late summer.	Sun to part shade; dry soil OK. Zone 7	Can be sheared (although not tightly), but looks best when selectively pruned for height by cutting out stems instead so that foliage isn't damaged.
Cornus alba (redtwig dogwood)	Deciduous, suckering shrub 6 to 8 ft. high and spreading; stems bright to dark red.	Sun; takes wet soil. Zone 3	Beautiful winter aspect of glowing red bare stems. *C. sericea* and *C. sanguinea* are similar, with various cultivars.
Elaeagnus pungens (silverberry)	Evergreen shrub 10 ft. high and as wide; stems often thorny; leaves have wavy edges and tiny silver or brown dots that shimmer.	Full sun. Zone 7	Withstands shearing to become dense and twiggy. 'Maculata' has gold-centered leaves; 'St. Mary' grows to 6 ft. high and as wide, with small leaves.
Escallonia × langleyensis 'Apple Blossom' (Apple Blossom escallonia)	Evergreen shrub 5 ft. high and as wide; clusters of light pink flowers throughout the summer.	Full sun; summer dry soil OK. Zones 7–8	Attractive year-round; can be shaped. *E. rubra* reaches 10 ft.
Ilex crenata 'Beehive' (Beehive Japanese holly)	Evergreen shrub 4 ft. high and 5 ft. wide; small, dark green leaves; dense habit; male, therefore has no fruit.	Full sun. Zone 6	Conical shape, so can be used as is in a row or sheared for low hedge/divider; neat and tidy.
Ilex crenata 'Jersey Pinnacle' (Jersey Pinnacle Japanese holly)	Evergreen shrub 6 ft. high and 4 ft. wide; dense growth.	Full sun. Zone 6	Taller plant for more privacy; can be shaped but looks best left to its neat self.
Myrica californica (Pacific wax myrtle)	Evergreen shrub 10 ft. high and as wide; narrow leaves; flowers insignificant; dark berries on stems in fall.	Full sun or part shade; dry summer soil OK. Zone 7	Handsome plant; can be shaped; good for seaside plantings and windy places; fruit attractive to birds.
Osmanthus delavayi (Delavay osmanthus)	Evergreen shrub 6 ft. high and as wide; small, dark green leaves; clusters of small, fragrant white flowers in spring.	Full sun. Zone 8	Arching, mounding form will take shaping, or use unsheared for an informal hedge. Flowers smell like baby powder.

NAME	APPEARANCE	CULTURE	NOTES
Osmanthus heterophyllus (holly olive)	Evergreen shrub to 15 ft. high and 5 ft. wide; spiny, hollylike leaves; fragrant flowers in fall.	Full sun to part shade. Zone 7	Stiffly upright form lends itself to hedge. 'Goshiki' has foliage mottled yellow; 'Variegatus' has foliage marked with creamy white.
Prunus lusitanica (Portuguese laurel)	Evergreen tree 30 ft. high and 20 ft. wide; dark green foliage edged in red; white cones of flowers; black fruit.	Full sun. Zone 7	Beautiful tree in its own right, also takes shaping well; good cover and food for birds.
Rosa rugosa (tomato rose)	Deciduous; 4 to 5 ft. high and as wide; apple-green crinkled foliage on bristly stems; single or double flowers; fat red hips in fall.	Full sun. Zone 3	Provides four seasons of interest as an informal hedge; hips draw birds. *R. rugosa* 'Thérèse Bugnet' has ruffled, fragrant pink flowers; *R. rugosa* f. *alba* a fragrant white single; many other cultivars available.
Taxus baccata 'Fastigiata' (English yew)	Evergreen shrub/tree 15 to 30 ft. high; dense, dark green foliage.	Full sun to shade. Zone 7	Classic English hedge material; takes shearing perfectly and ends up looking solid. *T.* x *media* 'Hicksii', 10 to 20 ft., is also good for shearing.
Thuja occidentalis 'Brandon' (Brandon arborvitae)	Evergreen conifer 12 to 15 ft. high and 6 to 8 ft. wide.	Full sun. Zone 3	Other selections of arborvitae: 'Yellow Ribbon', 10 ft. high and 3 ft. wide, with yellow-orange new growth; 'Elegantissima', 10 to 15 ft. high and 4 to 5 ft. wide.
Thuja plicata 'Fastigiata' (Hogan columnar cedar)	Evergreen conifer 15 to 20 ft. high in narrow column; foliage has bronze cast in winter.	Full sun to part shade; takes dry summer soil. Zone 5	Select a narrow conifer for ultimate height; they look best when their tops aren't cut off.
Viburnum trilobum 'Wentworth' (Wentworth American cranberry bush)	Deciduous shrub 10 ft. high and 4 ft. wide; maple-shaped leaves; flat-topped clusters of white flowers, red berries.	Full sun to part shade. Zone 2	Red-tinged new growth and good fall color make this lively hedge material; birds will like the fruit. Dense, twiggy growth; no shearing needed.

Narrow Plants

Below: *Nandina domestica* 'Moyer's Red' is one of many heavenly bamboo cultivars that are suited to narrow spots.

Narrow plants can provide a vertical element in the garden, just as an obelisk or a birdhouse on a pole does. But in addition to making these exclamation points within the garden, narrow plants can fill in blank corners and line up along narrow paths. If you have a narrow site, the idea is to select a plant that works well for the space available, not choose one that you will have to continually snip and cut to fit. Apart from hedge plants, the natural form of a plant is one to be admired, not disguised. Gracefully arching branches that get headed back yearly to stubs grow into a twiggy mess that not only is unattractive but often weakens the plant.

Fortunately, there are plants to fit just about any space. More than placeholders, narrow plants add form and foliage to the overall design and feel of the garden.

NAME	APPEARANCE	CULTURE	NOTES
Azara microphylla (boxleaf azara)	Evergreen shrub/tree 20 ft. high and 8 ft. wide; small leaves on horizontal branches; tiny but fragrant flowers late winter/early spring.	Part shade; protect from winds. Zone 8	Airy foliage makes a nice scrim. Plant in a quiet corner near a doorway to enjoy winter fragrance; if there's room, plant three for more effect.
Berberis thunbergii 'Helmond Pillar' (Helmond Pillar Japanese barberry)	Deciduous shrub 4 ft. tall and 2 ft. wide; dark purple foliage turns bright red in fall.	Full sun. Zone 4	Dark purple is a good foil to orange and yellow; single plant makes a statement, several can form their own fence.
Buxus sempervirens 'Graham Blandy' (Graham Blandy English boxwood)	Evergreen shrub 8 ft. high and 1 ft. wide; small leaves dark green, with new growth more yellow.	Part shade. Zone 5	One of the narrowest English boxwoods, with a fine, stiff-upper-lip form.
Chamaecyparis nootkatensis 'Green Arrow' (Green Arrow Alaska cedar)	Evergreen conifer 30 ft. high and 5 ft. wide, irregularly branched.	Full sun to part shade. Zone 4	Like a marionette with branches upswept at the ends; striking, graceful effect, but don't plant it alone—it looks better with shrubs nearby.

NAME	APPEARANCE	CULTURE	NOTES
Eucryphia x *nymansensis* 'Mt. Usher' (Mt. Usher eucryphia)	Evergreen tree, 20 ft. high and 8 ft. wide; 2-inch white flowers in late summer.	Part shade; dry summer soil OK. Zone 8	Handsome small tree; plant it to enjoy the flowers, but avoid the bees. *E.* x *intermedia* 'Rostrevor' has similar form and flowers but is deciduous.
Fagus sylvatica 'Dawyck Purple' (Dawyck Purple European beech)	Deciduous tree to 60 ft. high but barely 10 ft. wide; purple foliage turns bronze in summer.	Full sun. Zone 5	Lovely slender look turns terrible if top is cut off to "control size," so plant only if it has headroom.
Ginkgo biloba 'Mayfield' (Mayfield maidenhair tree)	Deciduous tree to 40 ft. high and 8 ft. wide; apple-green leaves with distinctive fern shape.	Full sun. Zone 4	Interesting texture for a tree; good for an entry or corner of back garden; fall color is buttery yellow, but leaves fall in a short time.
Ilex crenata 'Sky Pencil' (Sky Pencil Japanese holly)	Evergreen shrub to 10 ft. high and 8 in. wide (really).	Full sun. Zone 5	An exclamation point for the garden or planter; use three in a row if it's too skinny or if you need a short section of screen. Sometimes listed as 'Sky Sentry'.
Juniperus scopulorum 'Skyrocket' (columnar juniper)	Evergreen conifer 20 ft. high and 3 ft. wide; blue-green, dense foliage.	Full sun; well-drained soil. Zone 5	An interesting pencil-thin statement. Well-drained soil is a must or junipers will die of root rot.
Malus (apple) 'North Pole' 'Golden Sentinel' 'Scarlet Sentinel'	Deciduous fruiting trees to 9 ft. high and 1 ft. wide; fruit colors are red, yellow, and yellow with red blush respectively.	Full sun. Zone 4	Beanpole apple trees—made to order for the small garden.
Nandina domestica (heavenly bamboo)	Evergreen shrub 4 to 6 ft. high; airy foliage on slender stems; upright clusters of flowers turn to red berries; fall and winter foliage various shades of red.	Full sun to shade; dry summer soil OK. Zone 6	Straight species is more narrow-growing than many cultivars; offers bare stems at base where you can plant a small-scale ground cover.
Pyrus calleriana 'Chanticleer' (columnar ornamental pear)	Deciduous tree 35 ft. high and 10 ft. wide; clusters of white flowers in spring; fall color orange to purple.	Full sun. Zone 5	Good spring bloom and fall color, but it's not a fruiting variety.
Thuja occidentalis 'Holmstrup' (Holmstrup arborvitae)	Evergreen conifer 10 ft. high and 2 ft. wide; vertically held fans of foliage.	Full sun to part shade. Zone 3	Good backdrop for winter berries such as *Callicarpa*; year-round no-fuss plant. See also *T. plicata* 'Fastigiata' (in "Hedges" list).

Perennials

You may wonder how a list of perennials for the small garden differs from one for a larger garden—are these all tiny plants? It's good to know that you needn't choose only diminutive flowers; a 6-foot giant kale *(Crambe cordifolia)* may suit your small garden just fine. All the plants listed here have been chosen for their good looks over a long period. Some are notable for extended bloom; others have an attractive appearance when out of flower; and at the very least, there are those that don't make a nuisance out of themselves when their flowering time is finished.

The concept of mixed plantings is particularly important in the small garden. Most perennials are herbaceous, meaning that they disappear completely over winter. Others may leave behind an evergreen base of leaves, which helps keep the garden from looking devastated, but a still better plan is to incorporate perennials among plantings of shrubs and under trees. Perennials in pots can be mixed with woody plants, too. Or, if grouped in their own pots, they can be rearranged so that they are front and center when they look best.

Below: **Many geraniums bloom all summer long.**

NAME	APPEARANCE	CULTURE	NOTES
Aster divaricatus (wood aster)	Wiry, relaxed stems to 3 ft., spreading, wandering; small white flowers late summer into fall.	Shade; dry summer soil OK. Zone 6	Perfect weaver for the shade garden; masses of flowers brighten up dark spots.
Aster × frikartii 'Mönch'	Forms clumps 2 ft. high and wider than it is tall; lavender-blue daisylike flowers all summer.	Full sun. Zone 5	Easy care with a long season of bloom.
Astilbe × arendsii	Ferny foliage; 2 to 4 ft. high (including flower stems) and as wide; selections available to bloom from spring to late summer.	Part shade to shade; regular water. Zone 5	Feathery plumes add color to shady areas. 'Rheinland' early, dark pink flowers; 'Peach Blossom' mid; 'Bridal Veil' late white; 'Pumila' to 8 in., late, pink flowers.
Begonia grandis (hardy begonia)	To 3 ft. high and slender; leaves asymmetrical, spotted, red underneath; clusters of white to pink flowers in summer.	Part shade. Zone 7	Try to position it so the sun comes from behind— the red-backed leaves glow.
Boltonia asteroides 'Snowbank' (Snowbank boltonia)	To 4 ft. high, in airy mounds; small, white daisylike flowers in autumn.	Full sun to part shade. Zone 3	You won't even notice it growing through the summer, and then suddenly, when the season is almost over, it rises to the occasion with masses of flowers. 'Pink Beauty' is also nice.
Chrysanthemum 'Sheffield' (Sheffield chrysanthemum)	Clumps of foliage 30 in. high and as wide; apricot flowers in fall.	Full sun; dry summer soil OK. Zone 4	Good-looking hardy mum has the florist types beat. C. × *rubellum* 'Clara Curtis', with pink flowers, blooms late summer into fall.
Coreopsis verticillata (threadleaf tickweed)	To 18 in. high, clumps up to 2 ft. across; dark, soft, thin foliage; light to dark yellow daisylike flowers all summer.	Full sun; dry summer soil OK. Zone 5	Airy appearance in summer is good foil to big-leaved plants. 'Moonbeam' has light yellow flowers, 'Zagreb' dark yellow. C. *rosea* has pink flowers.
Corydalis lutea (yellow corydalis)	Ferny foliage in clumps to 1 ft. high and 2 ft. wide; clusters of small yellow flowers all summer.	Sun to part shade; dry summer soil OK. Zone 6	Great container plant as it billows over edges; reseeds and charmingly comes up in pavement cracks (which may try the patience of some gardeners).
Disporum hookeriana (fairy bells)	Arching stems to 2 ft.; spreads underground; small, dangling white flowers in spring followed by orange berries.	Shade; dry summer soil OK. Zone 7	Other similar spring-flowering woodland plants that brighten up dark walks: *Smilacina racemosa* (Solomon's seal) to 3 ft.; S. *stellata* to 2 ft.

NAME	APPEARANCE	CULTURE	NOTES
Erigeron karvinskianus 'Profusion' (Profusion fleabane)	Spreading clumps of foliage to 9 in. high and 3 ft. wide; small white/pink daisies all summer.	Full sun. Zone 5	Excellent, unobtrusive plant that nestles up against other perennials; also good in containers as a trailer.
Erysimum 'Bowles Mauve' (Bowles Mauve wallflower)	Evergreen shrubby mounds 3 ft. high and as wide; gray-green foliage; stems of dark mauve flowers.	Full sun; summer dry soil OK. Zone 7	Blooms constantly, almost year-round, for three years and then dies; take cuttings or buy a new one.
Eupatorium cannabinum 'Flore Pleno' (double-flowered agrimony)	Narrow plant with stems 4 to 5 ft., topped with masses of tiny mauve flowers in summer.	Full sun. Zone 5	Does not reseed as does the species. *E. fistulum* 'Gateway' reaches 6 ft. or more; flowers bright pink.
Euphorbia dulcis 'Chameleon' (Chameleon spurge)	Clumps of dark chocolate stems to 2 ft.; flowers tiny but surrounded by lime-yellow bracts.	Full sun or part shade. Zone 5	Cut plant back when it blooms for fresh growth (and to avoid having a million seedlings). *E. griffithii* 'Dixter' grows 2 to 3 ft. with orange flower stems; 'Fireglow' is orange-red.
Gaura lindheimeri	Airy clumps to 3 ft. high and as wide; long flower stems weave among other plants; white flowers over a long season.	Full sun; summer dry soil OK. Zone 5	Looks good cascading down a slope. 'Siskiyou Pink' has dark pink flowers.
Geranium x *riversleaianum* 'Mavis Simpson' 'Russell Pritchard'	Low mounds of foliage; scalloped gray-green leaves; light pink and magenta flowers, respectively, over a long period.	Full sun or part shade. Zone 5	So many geraniums, so little space! These bloom continously in summer. *G. pratense* 'Victor Reiter' has dark, deeply cut foliage and blue flowers.
G. sanguineum (bloody cranesbill)	Small, deeply scalloped leaves on clumping plants to 12 in. high and 2 ft. wide; magenta flowers in late spring.	Sun to part shade. Zone 5	Cut whole plant back after blooming for rebloom in fall. 'Album' has white flowers.
Geum rivale (water avens)	Basal rosette of long, scalloped leaves to 1 ft. wide; flower stems to 1 ft.; nodding copper flowers in spring.	Full sun to part shade; takes damp soil. Zone 5	Will rebloom if all spent flower stems are cut back. Other geums: 'Lady Stratheden', double yellow flowers; 'Red Wings', double deep red flowers; 'Georgenburg', single apricot flowers with red back.

NAME	APPEARANCE	CULTURE	NOTES
Heuchera spp. (coral bells)	To 1 ft. high and 18 in. across; wide, lobed leaves sometimes evergreen; thin stalks to 2 ft. with tiny white or red flowers.	Part shade (cultivars of *H. sanguinea* take full sun). Zones 4–5	Fine tall ground covers. Dark-foliaged forms include 'Chocolate Ruffles' and 'Stormy Seas'.
Hosta spp.	Herbaceous clumps of foliage up to 4 ft. across with variously blue-green, green, or variegated leaves; in summer, flower stems to 3 ft., white or lavender, some fragrant.	Part shade. Zone 5	You could have an entire hosta garden and no two plants alike: *H. sieboldiana* var. *elegans* has gray-green seersucker leaves; *H. plantaginea* has fragrant white flowers; *H. plantaginea* 'June' has leaves mottled blue-green.
Iris—Pacific Coast hybrids	Evergreen foliage in grassy clumps; spring flowers in shades of lavender-blue, purple, gold, and rasp-berry, many with varied markings.	Full sun to part shade; no need to plant rhizomes at soil level as is required with bearded iris; summer dry soil OK. Zone 7	Fabulous easy-care iris with stunning beauty; even clumps of foliage look good. Colors often unselected at nurseries, but it doesn't matter— they're all beautiful.
Lilium hybrids (oriental lily)	Stalks to 5 ft.; trumpet flowers in midsummer to fall, many with recurved petals; highly fragrant.	Full sun to part shade; high organic matter, regular water and fertilizer. Zone 5	Exotic but fussy, so plant these in pots with annuals that also need attention.
Meconopsis cambrica (Welsh poppy)	Basal rosette of deeply cut leaves, yellow to orange cupped flowers, on stems to 1 ft., open from fuzzy heads in spring.	Part shade. Zone 6	Reseeds, but it's so lovely that some gardeners make a point of sprinkling the seed around.
Nepeta cultivars (catmint)	Gray-green foliage in clumps 1 to 3 ft.; summer bloom of lavender-blue flowers.	Full sun. Zones 4–5	Plant against a hot wall; blues cool off brassy yellows and oranges. Cut flower stems back for rebloom. 'Walker's Low' 15 in., lavender flowers; 'Six Hills Giant' 3 ft.
Origanum 'Kent Beauty' (ornamental oregano)	Rounded leaves on clumps of foliage to 6 in. high and 8 in. wide; pink, hoplike flowers all summer.	Full sun; dry summer soil OK. Zone 7	It's small, so don't let it disappear. For larger effect, try *O. laevigatum* 'Herrenhausen', 2 ft. tall and 3 ft. wide, with domed clusters of mauve flowers.
Paeonia spp. (peony)	Variously ferny foliage; clumps to 4 ft. high and as wide; single or double flowers in white and shades of pink and red in early summer.	Full sun; do not plant too deep nor apply mulch on top of dormant plant. Zone 5	Nice foliage, too, so there's interest after flowering. The classics are 'Sarah Bernhardt' (double pink) and 'Festiva Maxima' (white with raspberry flecks).

NAME	APPEARANCE	CULTURE	NOTES
Penstemon (garden hybrids)	Shrubby growth to 3 ft. high and as wide, often evergreen; narrow leaves; foxglove-shaped flowers in early summer and fall.	Full sun; summer dry soil OK. Zone 7	Cut back faded flower stems for second flush. Many cultivars include 'Garnet' (claret), 'Blackbird' (purple-black), and 'Apple Blossom' (light pink).
Persicaria amplexicaulis 'Firetail'	Large clumps 2 to 4 ft. high and as wide; bright red spires of flowers in late summer.	Full sun. Zone 5	Sizable, but worth it for nonstop, late-summer display.
Phlox paniculata (summer phlox)	2 to 3 ft. high, spreading almost as wide; fragrant flowers in summer.	Full sun to light shade. Zone 5	Powdery mildew always a problem, but worth it for flowers, fragrance, and old-fashioned look. 'Mt. Fuji' white; 'Franz Schubert' lilac.
Phygelius x *rectus* (Cape fuchsia)	Shrubby, semi-evergreen plants to 3 ft. high and as wide; summer flowers are narrow and tubular.	Full sun; dry summer soil OK. Zone 7	Runs some, so don't coddle. 'African Queen' is salmon, 'Moonraker' pale yellow, 'Winchester Fanfare' coral with yellow throat, 'Trewidden Pink' pink.
Pulmonaria spp. (lungwort)	Clumps of foliage to 1 ft. high and as wide; long leaves, often spotted white; clusters of early spring flowers, some two-toned.	Shade. Zone 4	Valuable to brighten shady spots in spring. Prevent powdery mildew by cutting off all old foliage and spent flower stems to let new growth emerge. *P. saccharata* 'Roy Davidson' is light blue; 'Sissinghurst White' is white.
Solidago rugosa 'Fireworks' (Fireworks goldenrod)	To 4 ft. high, but keeping to tight clumps; slightly hairy leaves; bright yellow flowers in late summer.	Full sun. Zone 3	Bright and lively show late in the season; birds enjoy the seeds. Give plants full sun or you'll need to stake them. 'Golden Baby' grows to 2 ft.

Shrubs

Often, we choose shrubs with a particularly stunning season—outstanding bloom in spring, for example—that fade into the background of the border when their show is over. If we are especially attracted to a wild spring show, however, we could end up with a floriferous May, a drab August, and a dreary December. For the small garden, and particularly for areas that you see in at least three seasons, choose some shrubs for their winter merit: a handsome bare profile, attractively peeling bark, or fruit that hangs on. Make sure that the bulk of the foliage you see in August doesn't look tired. Three rhodies in a row may knock your socks off when they're in full bloom in May, but your interest flags soon after, when they settle into their rangy three-season doldrums. Instead, group three different shrubs—a compact, pink-flowered rhododendron (both 'Christmas Cheer' and 'Cilpinense' grow to 3 to 4 feet and bloom in mid- to late winter), a creamy-white variegated *Euonymus fortunei* 'Emerald Gaiety', and the quiet presence of a narrow, 6-foot evergreen boxwood (*Buxus* 'Graham Blandy')—and you'll have something to admire year-round.

Below: **Mrs. Robb's spurge** (*Euphorbia amygdaloides var. robbiae*) **provides a much-needed evergreen presence.**

NAME	APPEARANCE	CULTURE	NOTES
Aesculus parviflora (bottlebrush buckeye)	Deciduous, 10 ft. high, 15 ft. wide; suckering, with white bottlebrush flowers in summer and horse chestnut–like leaves.	Sun or part shade; takes clay soil. Zone 4	Gives a vertical look to plantings, so grow this with other, fuller plants in front; you can reduce its size by cutting out whole stems to the ground.
Amelanchier alnifolia (serviceberry)	Deciduous; 12 ft. high and as wide; often multi-stemmed; strappy white flowers in spring; summer fruit resembles blueberries; yellow fall color.	Full sun or part shade; dry soil in summer OK. Zone 4	Northwest native; spring and summer interest; in winter has a nice gray, twiggy effect. Good hedgerow plant, provides food for birds.
Arbutus unedo (strawberry tree)	Evergreen; 25 ft. high and as wide; glossy dark green foliage; small white bell-shaped flowers in late fall and winter at same time as round, bumpy red fruit.	Full sun; dry soil in summer OK. Zone 7	Large, mounding tree/shrub; limb it up so you can see its beautiful cinnamon-colored bark. 'Compacta' to 10 ft., 'Elfin King' to 6 ft.
Berberis thunbergii 'Crimson Pygmy' (crimson pygmy barberry)	Deciduous; 2 ft. high and as wide, bright-red new growth, turning more bronze in summer; thorny stems; yellow flowers; red fruit.	Full sun; takes clay soil. Zone 4	Good for informal barrier hedges or as an accent among all-green plants. 'Concorde' is 18 in. high with deep purple foliage.
B. x *stenophylla* 'Irwinii' (Irwin rosemary barberry)	Evergreen; 3 ft. high and as wide; thorny stems; clusters of yellow flowers in late spring, blue berries later.	Full sun; takes clay soil. Zone 7	Glossy leaves make a year-round statement; flowers and fruit add to the show.
Brachyglottis greyi	Evergreen; 3 ft. high and as wide; gray leaves with a silver edge; yellow daisy-like flowers in summer.	Full sun; dry soil OK. Zone 7	Cool look for a hot spot. Foliage is its best quality, not flowers.
Callicarpa dichotoma 'Issai' (Issai beautyberry)	Deciduous; 4 ft. high and as wide; arching branches; showy clusters of lavender berries all winter.	Full sun. Zone 4	It's a nondescript shrub most of the year, but plant this as a winter spotlight, with herbaceous perennials around it and a dark green conifer as a backdrop to set off the fruit.
Caryopteris x *clandonensis* (bluebeard)	Deciduous; 3 ft. high and as wide; gray-green leaves come out in late spring; small, fuzzy blue flowers in late summer.	Full sun; dry soil OK. Zone 5	Flowers are a good contrast to yellows and oranges in late-summer gardens. 'Dark Knight' has deep purple flowers, 'Longwood Blue' violet-blue flowers.

NAME	APPEARANCE	CULTURE	NOTES
Clethra alnifolia (sweet pepperbush)	Deciduous, upright, suckering, to 6 ft. high and as wide; glossy leaves; spires of white fragrant flowers in midsummer.	Part shade in evenly moist to damp soil. Zone 4	Spicy fragrance in late summer wafts on the warm breeze. Plant this where it will get watered. 'Hummingbird' grows to 4 feet; 'Ruby Spice' has deep pink flowers.
Deutzia gracilis (slender deutzia)	Deciduous; 3 ft. high and as wide; thin black stems and narrow, bright green leaves; clusters of fragrant white star-shaped flowers in spring.	Full sun. Zone 5	Spring flowers and fall color along with attractive summer foliage give three seasons of interest. *D. crenata* 'Nikko' grows to only 2 ft. and can be used as a high ground cover.
Disanthus cercidifolius	Multistemmed, 6 to 10 ft. high and as wide; heart-shaped leaves turn orange, claret, and purple in fall; inconspicuous flowers in fall.	Part shade to shade; prefers soil high in organic matter. Zone 7	Broader than some shrubs, but readily fits in with other plants because of its sparse growth and slender stems.
Enkianthus campanulatus	Deciduous; 8 ft.; narrow; clusters of heatherlike creamy flowers dangle from branches in spring; red fall foliage color.	Part shade, evenly moist acid soil. Zone 6	Narrow vase-shaped shrub with elegant look; provide some sun protection (trees above, or afternoon shade from a building). 'Red Bells' has particularly red veins in flowers.
Euphorbia amygdaloides var. *robbiae* (Mrs. Robb's spurge)	Evergreen; 2 to 3 ft. high and as wide; glossy leaves; yellow bouffant flower stems in early summer.	Part shade to shade; takes dry soil. Zone 7	Neat foliage and tolerance for dry shade make this a good year-round plant for difficult places. Dig up runners (there'll be few if it isn't over-cared-for).
Fuchsia magellanica (hardy fuchsia)	Deciduous; cultivars range from tiny to 4 ft. high and as wide; glossy foliage is slow to leaf out; bears summer to fall flowers on arching stems.	Full sun to afternoon shade; takes dry soil in summer. Zone 8	Vast number of cultivars to suit any garden. 'Peter Pan' to 8 in.; 'Chillerton Beauty' has large pink and violet flowers; 'Riccartonii' has masses of small dark red and purple flowers.
Fothergilla gardenii	Deciduous; 2 ft. high and as wide; early-spring bottle-brush flowers are vanilla-scented; good fall color.	Sun to part shade. Zone 5	Sweet and unassuming—tuck one or several into small spaces. Fall color is better in sun.

NAME	APPEARANCE	CULTURE	NOTES
Hydrangea quercifolia (oakleaf hydrangea)	Deciduous, suckering; 3 to 4 ft. high and as wide; oakleaf-shaped foliage; cones of white flowers in late summer; burgundy fall color.	Part shade to shade; takes some summer dryness in shade. Zone 5	Fabulous four-season plant with highlights in late summer (flowers) and fall (leaf color); brightens up dark places, never out of control. Shady side of garden would be great.
Lagerstroemia 'Pecos' (pink crape myrtle)	Deciduous; 8 ft. high and 6 ft. wide; new growth flushed bronze; conical clusters of flowers in late summer; maroon fall color.	Full sun. Zone 7	Choose a multistemmed plant for more impact— the bark peels and stems become marbled pink and brown; a fabulous shrub. 'Petite Embers' to 5 ft., with red flowers; 'Acoma' to 10 ft. high and as wide, with white flowers; many more cultivars.
Leucothoë fontanesiana (drooping leucothoë)	Evergreen; 3 to 4 ft. high and as wide; arching/drooping branches; pendulous clusters of white flowers in spring.	Shade; prefers even moisture but will take some summer dryness if not otherwise stressed. Zone 6	Elegant shrub for shade. 'Rainbow' has foliage mottled white and pink. Foliage of *L. axillaris* turns red in winter.
Lonicera nitida (box honeysuckle)	Evergreen; 4 feet high and as wide; small leaves give neat appearance; flowers insignificant.	Sun to part shade. Zone 6	Good accent for containers (it's slow-growing), entries, and the edges of courtyards. 'Baggesen's Gold' has yellow-tinged foliage; 'Silver Beauty' is white-edged; 'Red Tip' has red new growth.
Lonicera pileata (privet honeysuckle)	Evergreen; 2 to 3 ft; horizontal branches; small leaves; insignificant flowers.	Sun to part shade. Zone 6	Outstanding, handsome year-round look; horizontal branches are a good contrast to other plant shapes. Can be used as a low, informal hedge. Don't shear!
Mahonia nervosa (longleaf mahonia)	Evergreen to 3 ft.; long, compound leaves similar to holly; early-spring stems of bright yellow flowers followed in summer by blue berrylike fruit; claret-colored winter tones.	Part shade to shade; takes dry summer soil. Zone 6	Four-season plant for dry shade; looks fabulous all the time.

NAME	APPEARANCE	CULTURE	NOTES
Rhododendron yakushimanum cultivars	Evergreen, up to 4 ft. high and as wide; soft fuzziness on undersides of leaves; flowers in spring various shades of pink.	Part shade. Zones 5–6	Foliage looks good all year—don't settle for rhodies that look awful after they bloom. A series of cultivars are named after Disney's Seven Dwarfs (Sneezy, Doc, etc.); other cvs. are 'Yaku Princess' and 'Ken Janeck'. *R.* 'Lucy Lou' has white flowers and hairy leaves.
Ribes sanguineum (red flowering currant)	Deciduous; 8 ft. high and 4 ft. wide; upright growth; deep pink pendent clusters of flowers in early spring; blue berries follow.	Sun; takes dry summer soil OK. Zone 5	Long spring flower show is outstanding; birds enjoy the fruits. 'King Edward VII' is compact with red flowers; many other cultivars.
Sambucus nigra f. *laciniata* (cutleaf elderberry)	Deciduous; 8 to 12 ft. high and 5 ft. wide; deeply dissected leaves; flat-topped clusters of white flowers in late spring; black fruit.	Full sun to part shade. Zone 4	Fine texture sets off the foliage and flowers of other plants, but this shrub is so good-looking, it could stand alone.
Syringa laciniata (cutleaf lilac)	Deciduous; 8 ft. high and as wide; open, branching habit; clusters of fragrant lavender flowers along stems in spring.	Full sun. Zone 5	Fragrance of common lilac, but the deeply lobed foliage of this species looks good in summer too. Flowers disappear among leaves after bloom. A fine lilac for small gardens.
Viburnum x *bodnantense* 'Dawn' (fragrant Dawn viburnum)	Deciduous; 10 ft. high and 6 ft. wide; pleated leaves; clusters of intensely fragrant pink flowers in winter.	Full sun. Zone 6	For smaller effect, still with fragrance, try *V. farreri* 'Nanum', 2 to 3 ft. high and as wide.
Viburnum x *burkwoodii*	Semi-evergreen; 10 ft. high and 6 ft. wide; glossy foliage, white underneath; clusters of fragrant light pink flowers in late winter.	Full sun. Zone 6	Excellent and handsome shrub to train on an arbor that you walk through frequently—every pass a delicious sniff.
Viburnum plicatum f. *tomentosum* 'Shoshoni'	Deciduous; 5 ft. high and 8 ft. wide; horizontal branches with pleated leaves; red-purple fall color; clusters of white flowers; red to black fruit.	Full sun to part shade. Zone 5	Flowers appear along the branches in spring like epaulets; good structure. 'Summer Snowflake' has white lacecap flowers throughout the summer.

Small Conifers

Evergreens establish permanence in the garden. They are there throughout the year, before and after the fading glory of flowers and the progression of life evident in deciduous woody plants.

When we think of planting an evergreen, the native Northwest conifers come to mind—Western red cedar, Western hemlock, and Douglas fir. These can be huge, towering trees in the small garden. But there is a vast selection of dwarf and miniature conifer cultivars that fit into a garden of any size, and they can reflect whatever style you want to present. Planted in a row, tight, bun-shaped conifers present a formal, tidy look; dotted here and there among mixed plantings of trees, shrubs, and herbaceous plants, they offer a more casual appearance. Wherever they appear, they are handsome and low-maintenance. They make perfect backdrops for the more colorful members of the garden; whether it be a clump of purple coneflowers or a redtwig dogwood, any color stands out better when you put a conifer behind it.

The small conifers in this list range from 1 foot high to 10 feet high; some may eventually reach 25 feet. Most conifers grow slowly, so an ultimate height of even 10 feet can take a plant many years to attain.

Below: **Variegated false arborvitae (***Thujopsis dolobrata***'Variegata') adds texture to any planting.**

NAME	APPEARANCE	CULTURE	NOTES
Abies koreana 'Horstmann's Silberlocke' (Silver Korean fir)	Broadly upright 5 to 10 ft.; needles have white undersides and are upswept, giving plant an overall silvery appearance.	Full sun. Zone 5	Stiffly formal; an eye-catching color.
Abies pinsapo (Spanish fir)	Narrow to 25 ft. high; symmetrical form; needles stiff and radially arranged; cones point upward.	Full sun to part shade; dry soil OK. Zone 7	Hedgehog-like branches add interesting texture; form is pleasingly regular. Tree is much taller in nature (100 ft.!).
Chamaecyparis nootkatensis 'Glauca Compacta' (compact blue Alaska cedar)	Blue-green fans of foliage; grows to 6 ft. high and as wide, slowly.	Full sun. Zone 5	Alaska cedar is known for its loose, graceful sprays of draping foliage that turn up at the ends.
Chamaecyparis obtusa 'Filicoides' (fernspray false cypress)	Dark green sprays of foliage; grows to 6 ft. high and 3 ft. wide, slowly.	Full sun. Zone 5	Octopuslike arms rise up and out; good foil to mounding plants.
C. obtusa 'Nana Gracilis' (Nana Gracilis Hinoki cypress)	Dark green congested foliage; upright growth; to 3 to 6 ft.; broadly conical.	Full sun to part shade. Zone 5	Dense, dark foliage serves as backdrop for flowers, but its winter presence is just as important.
C. obtusa 'Kosteri' (Koster's Hinoki cypress)	Irregular pyramid to 3 ft. high and as wide, slow-growing; dark, twisted sprays of foliage.	Full sun. Zone 5	Congested foliage in layers like fluffy green cake frosting.
C. obtusa 'Mariesii' (variegated Hinoki cypress)	Irregular globe shape to 3 to 5 ft.; creamy white variegation.	Full sun. Zone 5	Variegation adds another dimension to the usefulness of conifers. 'Nana Lutea' has yellow-suffused foliage year-round.
C. pisifera 'Lemon Thread'	Broadly upright; 3 to 5 ft. high and almost as wide; yellow whipcord foliage.	Full sun. Zone 5	'Compacta Variegata' has irregular gold variegation.
Cryptomeria japonica 'Elegans Nana' (dwarf Japanese cedar)	Feathery, soft foliage, to 3 ft. high and as wide.	Full sun. Zone 6	'Pygmaea' 3 to 5 ft., broadly upright; 'Black Dragon' 15 ft. high and 7 ft. wide with dark, congested foliage.
Pinus contorta 'Spaan's Dwarf' (dwarf shore pine)	Broadly upright to 8 ft.; short, dense, dark green foliage.	Full sun. Zone 7	Small version of the shore pine; a good, solid green for the small garden.
Pinus strobus 'Nana' (Eastern dwarf white pine)	Dense plant, 3 to 7 ft. high and almost twice as wide.	Full sun. Zone 3	Almost like a tall ground cover; use this in a corner or along a fence and plant color around it.

NAME	APPEARANCE	CULTURE	NOTES
Pinus thunbergii 'Thunderhead' (dwarf Japanese black pine)	Broadly spreading to 10 ft. high and as wide; dark green needles; white "candles" in spring.	Full sun. Zone 5	Interesting contrast of white candles (new growth) against dark foliage. Pines seem to add age to a garden, even when the tree is young.
Taxus baccata 'Repandens' (spreading English yew)	Mounds of dark foliage, arching stems; 1 to 2 ft. high and up to 15 ft. wide.	Full sun to part shade. Zone 6	Can be treated as a tall ground cover; especially good for areas you can't reach easily to maintain.
Thujopsis dolobrata 'Variegata' (variegated false arborvitae)	Scalelike thick foliage, splashed with white; to 10 to 15 ft. high, 8 ft. wide, slow-growing; conical habit.	Full sun. Zone 5	Unusual texture, with foliage similar to Western red cedar but thicker leaves. 'Nana' is flat-topped, to 30 in. high and several feet wide.
T. mertensiana (mountain hemlock)	Soft mid-green foliage; 20 to 30 ft. high and 10 ft. wide.	Part shade. Zone 4	Soft, elegant look; long and short branches are mixed, giving it a disheveled but charming appearance.

Trees

When we learn that a "small" tree can grow up to 30 feet, most of us are shocked. That big? Maybe 30 feet can be considered small in comparison to a 200-foot Douglas fir. But in reality, when we're standing next to a tree, it's the tree's bulk—how dense the foliage is—that makes it feel "big." A slender Stewartia monadelpha or even a wide but see-through Parrotia persica can seem smaller than the dense, dark, rounded canopy of a 30-foot evergreen holm oak *(Quercus ilex).* And 30 feet isn't even as tall as a two-story house.

So, remember that you don't have to choose the tiniest tree in order to fit it into your small garden. It's wise to think about the height, but you need to also consider the growth form of the tree. Elbowroom is just as important as headroom.

Below: **The stark beauty of paperback maple** *(Acer griseum)* **is an addition to any winter landscape.**

NAME	APPEARANCE	CULTURE	NOTES
Acer crataegifolium (hawthorn maple)	To 20 ft.; broad, conical form; leaves shaped like those of hawthorn; bark faintly striped.	Part shade; this and other stripe-bark maples need to have the trunk shaded or they will scorch. Zone 6	Charming small tree for beside an entry or in the woodland side garden. 'Veitchii' has leaves . mottled white with occasional pink tones.
Acer griseum (paperbark maple)	To 25 ft.; broad columnar form; leaves divided into threes; fall colors orange, red, scarlet; peeling cinnamon-colored bark.	Full sun. Zone 4	A good tree to have outside the kitchen window, where its curling bark can be admired in bleak weather.
Acer japonicum (fullmoon maple)	Slowly to 30 ft.; broadly spreading, sometimes multitrunked; spring foliage bright green with drooping clusters of red flowers; good fall color.	Full to part sun but with some shelter. Zone 6	Plant where it will catch morning or late afternoon sun—and enjoy the fiery display of orange, maroon, and gold in fall. 'Aconitifolium' (fernleaf maple) has dissected leaves for a more refined look.
Acer tataricum var. *ginnala* (Amur maple)	To 30 ft. (at best); spreading form; glossy leaves notched into three lobes; red spring flowers are fragrant, fall color is flaming.	Full sun to part shade. Zone 3	Valuable for its foliage, attractive in summer and fall. Smaller cultivars: 'Compacta' to 10 ft., 'Emerald Elf' to 6 ft.
Amelanchier x *grandiflora* (serviceberry)	Spreading form to 25 ft.; often multitrunked; white flowers in spring, blue berries in summer, bright orange color in fall; winter twigs form a ruddy haze.	Full sun. Zone 4	Summer fruit for birds; plant along the fence of a shallow sunny border. Many cultivars; 'Robin Hill' is narrower, 'Brilliant' has more intense fall color.
x *Chitalpa tashkentensis*	Fast growth to about 25 ft.; spreading habit; late-summer flowers, white speckled with lavender, appear in clusters above the long, slender leaves.	Full sun; will take dry soils once established. Zone 6	Few trees bloom in summer, so place this where you'll enjoy it.
Cornus alternifolia (pagoda dogwood)	To 20 ft. high and as wide with spreading, horizontal branches in a tiered effect; insignificant spring flowers give way to black fruit, then good red fall color.	Part shade. Zone 3	Give it enough room to spread its branches, as these have a decided attraction in the winter garden. 'Argentea', with leaves edged in white, grows to only 10 ft. high and 8 ft. wide.

NAME	APPEARANCE	CULTURE	NOTES
Cornus kousa (Korean dogwood)	To 20 ft. or more over time, with a broadly columnar form; flowers in early summer; fruit bumpy, round, strawberry-colored, held upright; excellent fall color in shades of red.	Full sun. Zone 5	Good resistance to the dreaded dogwood anthracnose disease; one of the best small trees. Large "flowers" (really bracts) are white ('Milky Way', 'Moonbeam') or pink ('Satomi', 'Radiant Rose') and can be 4 or 5 in. across.
Magnolia sieboldii	Multistemmed, 15 to 20 ft. high and as wide; in late spring and sporadically through summer, large white flowers with center of red stamens open from fuzzy, upright buds.	Full sun to part shade. Zone 6	Magnificent in all respects. Clothe the base with low ground covers so that its attractive form isn't covered. Cup-shaped flowers up to 5 in. wide; berrylike clusters of red fruit held upright are yet another thing to love.
Malus sargentii (Sargent's crabapple)	Broadly spreading 15 to 20 ft.; usually wider than tall; green foliage; red buds open to white flowers in spring; clusters of small red fruit.	Full sun. Zone 4	Provides winter ornament and food for the birds. Grows wide, so give it a corner to itself so you won't have to cut to fit.
Malus cultivars (crabapple)	Broadly spreading, 15 to 20 ft.; green or purple foliage with good fall color; red or yellow fruit.	Full sun; choose a cultivar labeled "disease-resistant." Zone 4	'Christmas Holly' has red buds, white flowers, red fruit; 'Doubloons' has double white flowers, yellow fruit; 'Sugar Tyme' has pink buds, white flowers, red fruit on long stems that hang like cherries.
Ostrya virginiana (American hop hornbeam)	To 25 ft., slowly; pyramidal to round form; flowers small catkins; clusters of papery, hoplike fruits hold on in winter.	Full sun to part shade; takes clay soil. Zone 3	A lovely tree with fine texture and form; blends well with other plants and makes a fine backdrop for color.
Oxydendrum arboreum (sourwood tree)	Slow growth to about 25 ft. or more; narrow form; long, narrow, dark green leaves like peach foliage; drooping white clusters of flowers in midsummer; orange fall color.	Full sun or part shade; a member of the heath family, so prefers acid soil. Zone 6	A real showstopper in fall, with white flowers and shocking orange foliage.
Robina pseudoacacia 'Frisia' (golden-leaved locust)	To 30 ft.; chartreuse compound leaves and hanging clusters of white, fragrant flowers in spring.	Full sun or part shade (not dense). Zone 4	The golden yellow foliage lights up the scene spring through fall. Look out for thorns on branches.

NAME	APPEARANCE	CULTURE	NOTES
Sinojackia xylocarpa	To 15 ft.; white bells dangle from the branches in early summer.	Full sun to part shade. Zone 7	A lovely small tree to anchor the corner of a courtyard or woodland garden.
Stewartia monadelpha (tall stewartia)	To 25 ft. with broadly columnar form; white camellia-like flowers in early summer; peeling bark reveals mottled gray, pink, and brown.	Full sun to part shade. Zone 6	Glossy leaves turn reddish purple in autumn; a beautiful year-round tree, so don't stick it behind the garage where you'll never see it. *S. pseudocamellia* is similar, with larger flowers.

Variegated Plants

Variegated plants look best sprinkled throughout the garden, showing up between solid green plants and among flowers. They set off any plant combination, bringing life to a collection, adding a spark to a dark spot, and drawing the eye. Many different variegated plants grouped together, however, can be unsettling; their clashing patterns are too busy, and it's difficult to see anything clearly. Let variegation be the accessory, not the entire outfit.

Many variegated plants, often smaller-growing than other cultivars of the same species, are prime candidates for pots. Here, you can match or contrast the two- or three-tone color of the leaves, and when you play off the size and shapes in such close quarters there is a greater impact than if the variegation were in the middle of a bigger planting.

Variegated plants are a mixed lot when it comes to culture. Some need full sun to retain their variegation, others need shade or they will burn. The light recommendations may not be the same as for the straight species or for another, nonvariegated cultivar of the same species.

Below: **Variegated Solomon's seal (*Polygonatum odoratum* 'Variegatum') lights up a shady spot.**

NAME	APPEARANCE	CULTURE	NOTES
Abelia × *grandiflora* 'Confetti' (variegated abelia)	Deciduous shrub; 3 ft. high and as wide; foliage pink, white, and green; clusters of bell-shaped flowers in summer.	Full sun. Zone 6	Arching stems; prune out oldest ones every couple of years to refresh. 'Frances Mason' has green and gold foliage.
Aralia elata 'Variegata' (variegated Japanese angelica tree)	Suckering small tree to only 15 ft.; trunk has spiny protrusions; huge (2 feet and more) leaves that divide and divide grow straight from the trunk; leaflets edged in creamy white.	Full sun. Zone 4	Use this plant where its elegant form can be admired, but not so close that you'll get stuck by the spines as you work next to it.
Berberis thunbergii 'Golden Ring' (Golden Ring barberry)	Deciduous shrub to 4 ft. high and as wide; red-purple leaves with gold margins; yellow flowers followed by red berries.	Full sun. Zone 4	Gold rings develop after foliage emerges (and more so in hot sun); *Berberis* stems are thorny.
Cornus alba 'Elegantissima' ('Aureo-marginata') (variegated Tatarian dogwood)	Suckering, deciduous shrub 6 ft. high and as wide; dark red stems; leaves with deep margin of white; small clusters of flowers; white berries.	Full sun; doesn't mind wet soil. Zone 4	For more colorful stems, cut down in late winter every couple of years (this goes for all twig dogwoods). 'Gouchaltii' has gold and pink variegation; 'Spatheii' has yellow leaf margins.
Cornus florida 'Golden Nugget' (pink-flowering dogwood)	Deciduous small tree to 20 ft. high and as wide; leaves splashed with gold; pink flowers in spring.	Full sun to part shade. Zone 5	Bright lights on a small tree can liven up a corner. *C. kousa* 'Snowboy', to 15 ft., has creamy leaf edges with some yellow.
Daphne × *burkwoodii* 'Carol Mackie'	Evergreen shrub 3 to 4 ft. high and as wide; gold leaf margins; clusters of light pink, highly fragrant flowers in late spring.	Full sun or part shade. Zone 4	As with all daphnes, you can't pay enough attention to good drainage. A fine plant for open entries where perfume will grab you.
Euonymus fortunei 'Emerald Gaiety'	Evergreen mounding/ trailing shrub to 2 ft. high and spreading; leaves deeply margined white with occasional pink tones in winter.	Full sun. Zone 5	Accommodating plant makes any companion look better; will "climb" when grown up against a wall. 'Harlequin' has white and pink dotted leaves; 'Emerald 'n Gold' has yellow variegation.
Fuchsia 'Versicolor'	Deciduous shrub to 2 to 4 ft. high and as wide; leaves grayish, marked with white and pink; slender magenta-and-purple flowers all summer into fall.	Full sun to part shade. Zone 8	Good container plant, as its arching stems droop some; also listed as 'Tricolor'.

NAME	APPEARANCE	CULTURE	NOTES
Heuchera sanguinea 'Frosty' (Frosty coral bells)	Perennial to 1 ft. high and 2 ft. wide; evergreen rosette of leaves "frosted" with white; slender stalks with red flowers.	Full sun to part shade. Zone 5	Especially useful brightening up a shady spot along a walk or near a door. *H. x brizoides* 'Snowstorm' has leaves heavily sprinkled with white.
Hosta 'Albo-marginata'	Herbaceous clumping perennial to 1 ft. high and 2 ft. wide; leaves widely margined in white; stalks of lavender flowers to 2 ft.	Part shade to shade. Zone 5	Too many variegated hostas to mention; 'Patriot' has leaves with white border; 'June' has blue-green leaves edged in gold; 'Moonlight' has lime green leaves edged in white.
Hydrangea macrophylla 'Variegata' (variegated hydrangea)	Deciduous shrub 3 to 4 ft. high and as wide; leaves broadly margined in creamy white; lacecap flowers in late summer.	Part shade. Zone 6	Lacecaps are a delicate touch for this lovely shrub; flowers vary from pinkish to bluish depending on pH of soil (the more acid, the more blue). 'Quadricolor' has white, green, yellow, and lime leaves.
Hypericum androsaemum 'Gladys Brabazon'	Deciduous shrub 2 to 3 ft. high and as wide; leaves splashed with white; yellow flowers; fruits turn pink to red to black.	Full sun to part shade. Zones 6–7	Lots of things to look at on this shrub, so plant it near some solid green, such as a small conifer, so that you can see the colors better.
Phlox paniculata 'Nora Leigh'	Herbaceous perennial 3 to 4 ft. high; slowly spreading clumps; leaves deeply edged in white, topped by pink fragrant flowers in summer.	Full sun. Zone 5	Bright, tall, and fragrant—a hit for summer combinations.
Polygonatum odoratum 'Variegatum' (variegated Solomon's seal)	Herbaceous perennial with reddish stems to 2 ft.; leaves edged in white; small white bell-shaped flowers dangle from leaf axils.	Part shade to shade. Zone 5	Elegant woodland plant to combine with *Oxalis* and *Asarum* (wild ginger); spreads at pleasing rate by underground stems.
Sedum spectabile 'Frosty Morn'	Herbaceous perennial 18 in. high and 2 ft. wide; succulent foliage deeply margined in silvery white; tight clusters of light pink flowers in summer.	Full sun. Zone 5	So bright and white, you almost need sunglasses. Use with rich green, such as *Ilex crenata* (Japanese holly), and long-blooming hardy geraniums.

Vines and Climbers

Vines can weave among other plants, scramble over shrubs, or take the star role on an arbor or trellis. Those that weave or grow through shrubs need to be pruned or cut back carefully so that you don't also cut off or break stems on the supporting shrub. Vines in containers need regular attention and water, but many are well suited for pots on the deck or patio. The vines listed here, with a few exceptions, all grow less than 15 feet or so; those that grow longer are suitable for a long run of fence or deck railing but can easily overwhelm an arbor.

Many deciduous vines have fruits or seed heads that look good in autumn, but generally you'll see only bare stems throughout winter. Depending on the species, you may need to prune hard or only groom the vines. Pruning is always a concern for gardeners, especially with *Clematis*. Generally, the large-flowered, early summer *Clematis* bloom on old wood—that which grew the year before. These are the vines to groom by taking out dead stems and removing stems that have gone astray. Later-blooming *Clematis* bloom on the current year's growth and can be cut back hard in late winter. This makes the vine leaf out lower, so there is less bare stem.

Evergreen vines need their own tending, which usually amounts to cleaning out dead foliage and thinning the number of stems so that there will be more air circulation. Do this no later than the end of winter, or you may disturb nesting birds!

Below: **The green-white double flowers of *Clematis* 'Duchess of Edinburgh' create an intriquing scene.**

NAME	APPEARANCE	CULTURE	NOTES
Actinidia kolomikta (male kiwi)	Deciduous, to 20 ft.; wide leaves painted with cream and pink; no fruit.	Part shade. Zone 5	Showy vine for training on a wall. Kiwis come in male and female plants; male plant has showy foliage, especially 'Arctic Beauty'.
Billardiera longiflora	Evergreen, to 10 ft.; small, narrow leaves; small yellow trumpet-shaped flowers in summer fade to lavender; oblong lavender berries.	Sun to part shade. Zone 7	Intriguing but diminutive; plant up close so you can see the strange fruit. OK in containers.
Clematis alpina (alpine clematis)	Deciduous, to 10 ft.; bell-shaped blue flowers in spring.	Full sun, provided roots are "cool"; mulch well and/or keep a flat rock over root system. Zone 3	Small enough to grow on shrubs without engulfing them. *C. alpina* 'Constance' has rose-pink flowers; *C. macropetala* is similar but perhaps earlier.
Clematis, early and large-flowered	Deciduous, to 12 ft.; flowers up to 6 in. across bloom on last year's wood; may rebloom in fall.	Full sun with "cool" roots; regular water and weak applications of fertilizer every two weeks; groom when new growth starts by taking out dead twigs. Zone 5	'Belle of Woking' is double mauve, 'General Sikorski' blue, 'Hagley Hybrid' light mauve.
Clematis x *jackmanii*	Deciduous, to 10 ft.; masses of deep purple flowers summer to fall.	Same care as above; can be cut back hard in late winter. Zone 6	On arbor or gate, provides fabulous foil for yellow flowers in late summer. Too vigorous to grow on a shrub.
Clematis montana	Deciduous, to 25 ft.; leaves dissected; masses of white or pink flowers in spring.	Same care as above, but groom plant only; cutting back hard will delay flowering for a year. Zone 6	It's so beautiful you should willingly give up a fence or garage wall. *C. montana* var. *rubens* 'Tetrarose' has lilac-pink flowers, bronze foliage.
Clematis viticella hybrids	Deciduous, to 14 ft.; late summer flowers on current year's growth.	Same care as above; cut back to within 18 in. of ground in late winter to promote fuller growth. Zone 6	'Betty Corning' has lavender bells; 'Etoile Violette' is deep purple; 'Polish Spirit' is red-purple.
x *Fatshedera lizei* 'Media Picta'	Evergreen to 10 ft., intermediate between vine and shrub; wide leaves with center of gold.	Shade; best trained on wall. Zone 8	Hybrid between *Fatsia* and English ivy; well-behaved; lights up dark spaces.

NAME	APPEARANCE	CULTURE	NOTES
Parthenocissus henryana (silvervein creeper)	Deciduous, to 20 ft.; leaves divided into five fingers with silver strip in middle; orange fall color.	Part shade to shade; takes clay soil; tolerates some dryness. Zone 7	Beautiful vine for terrible conditions; let it attach suckers to wall or fence.
Rosa 'Dublin Bay'	To 10 ft.; red, semi-double flowers all summer.	Full sun. Zone 5	Entwine these red roses with yellow flowers of the annual canary vine (*Tropaeolum peregrinum*) on a pillar or an arbor.
Rosa 'Galway Bay'	To 10 ft.; deep pink flowers, blooms throughout the summer.	Full sun. Zone 5	Small combinations make big effects. Try these deep pink roses with purple Jackman clematis, or with coneflowers (*Echinacea purpurea*) growing at the base, or bright yellow *Crocosmia* 'Norwich Canary'.
Rosa 'New Dawn'	To 10 ft.; bears light pink, smallish, fragrant flowers constantly throughout late spring and summer.	Full sun. Zone 4	Pair on a trellis, arbor, or low fence with a dark red clematis such as 'Rouge Cardinal', or let it billow above mounds of lavender.
Rosa 'White New Dawn'	To 12 ft., with smallish, fragrant white flowers throughout the summer.	Full sun. Zone 5	Just as lovely as the pink version. If you prefer bigger flowers, go with 'Climbing Iceberg'.
Solanum crispum 'Glasnevin' (potato vine)	Sprawling, semi-evergreen shrub/vine to 10 ft; purple flowers with yellow eyes resemble potato/tomato flowers; blooms all summer.	Full sun. Zone 7	Tie up to trellis or wall, or let lax stems wander through other plants.
Tropaeolum tuberosum 'Ken Aslet'	Deciduous, 6 to 9 ft., blue-green foliage; tubular orange flowers summer into fall.	Full sun. Zones	Hummingbirds love this. Tender, so tuber may be killed by cold or soggy soil; dig up and store in the basement like dahlias.

The Gardens and the Gardeners

The author and photographer gratefully acknowledge the owners of the gardens that appear in this book.

Page II: The Thomas Allsopp garden. *Page X*: The Hoven garden. *Page 3:* The Lawrence garden. *Page 4:* The Elizabeth Jones garden. *Page 6:* The Virginia Hand garden. *Page 13:* The Virginia Hand garden. *Page 14:* The Knowles garden. *Page 17:* The Allan Neid garden. *Page 26:* The Forsyth-Mann garden. *Page 30:* The Hoven garden. *Page 33:* The Gjovaag garden. *Page 34:* The Bruce Whitaker garden. *Page 36:* The Hoven garden. *Page 43:* The Mark Henry garden. *Page 45:* The MacNab garden. *Page 46:* The Cindy Dack garden. *Page 50:* The Kuhn-Bressler garden. *Page 56:* The Dishman garden. *Page 57:* The Gjovaag garden. *Page 64:* The Gjovaag garden. *Page 66:* The Beverly Merryfield garden. *Page 70:* The Ferguson garden. *Page 73:* The Virginia Hand garden. *Page 74:* The Chaun garden. *Page 79:* The Reed garden. *Page 80:* The Knowles garden. *Page 82:* The Mark Henry garden. *Page 85:* The Parnicky garden. *Page 92:* The Annette Iverson garden. *Page 96:* The Ashton garden. *Page 100:* The Annette Iverson garden. *Page 103:* The Mark Henry garden. *Page 104:* The Mark Henry garden. *Page 108:* The Mark Henry garden. *Page 109:* The Codiac-Kirkham garden. *Page 110:* The Annette Iverson garden. *Page 114:* The Elizabeth Hallbaerg garden. *Page 118:* The Katherine Fuel garden. *Page 120:* The Judy Newton garden. *Page 121:* The Stephen Darling garden. *Page 130:* The Judy Newton garden. *Page 134:* The Stephen Darling garden. *Page 138:* The Mico garden. *Page 143:* The Elizabeth Hallbaerg garden. *Page 145:* The Allderdice garden. *Page 151:* The Virginia Hand garden. *Page 152:* The Virginia Hand garden. *Page 154:* The Gjovaag garden. *Page 161:* The Codiac-Kirkham garden. *Page 162:* The Gjovaag garden

Index